THE COMPLETE AIR FRYER COOKBOOK

Healthier & Delicious Alternative Recipes to Deep-Frying
(Fast, Delicious & Easy to Bake, Grill & Fry Recipes)

BY

Crystal Beagley

© Copyright 2019 By CRTSTAL BEAGLEY

All Rights Reserved

The content contained within this book may not be reproduced, duplicated or transmitted without direct written permission from the author or the publisher.

Under no circumstances will any blame or legal responsibility be held against the publisher or author, for any damages, reparation, or monetary loss due to the information contained within this book. Either directly or indirectly.

Legal Notice:-

This book is copyright protected. This book is only for personal use. You cannot amend, distribute, sell, use, quote or paraphrase any part, or the content within this book, without the consent or the author or publisher.

Disclaimer Notice:-

Please not the information contained within this document is for educational and entertainment purposes only. All effort has been executed to present accurate, up to date, and reliable, complete information. No warranties of any kind are declared or implied. Readers acknowledge that the author is not engaging in the rendering of legal, financial, medical or professional advice. The content within this book has been derived from various sources. Please consult a licensed professional before attempting any techniques outlined in this book.

By reading this document, the reader agrees that under no circumstances is the author responsible for any losses, direct or indirect, which are incurred as a result of the use of information contained within this document, including, but not limited to, - errors, omissions, or inaccuracies.

TABLE OF CONTENTS

INTRODUCTION 1

   BENEFITS OF USING THIS AIR FRYER COOKBOOK! 2

   WHY ARE YOU USE THIS AIR FRYER COOKBOOK? 4

EASY AIR FRYER RECIPES THAT CATER TO YOUR SPECIFIC NEEDS 5

   1. AIR FRIED PORK TAQUITOS 5

   2. AIR FRYER BREAKFAST FRITTATA 6

   3. CINNAMONROLLS 6

   4. CRISPY AVOCADO FRIES 8

   5. AIR FRYER BANANA BREAD 8

   6. CHURROS WITH CHOCOLATE SAUCE 9

   7. AIR-FRIED CINNAMON APPLE CHIPS WITH ALMOND YOGURT DIP 10

   8. BOURBON BACON BURGER 11

   9. AIR FRIED SWEET POTATO DESSERT FRIES 13

   10. ZESTY RANCH AIR FRYER FISH FILLETS 14

   11. AIR FRYER RASPBERRY BALSAMIC SMOKED PORK CHOPS 14

   12. AIR FRYER COCONUT SHRIMP WITH PIÑA COLADA DIP 15

   13. AIR-FRYER-GARLIC-ROSEMARY BRUSSELS SPROUTS 16

   14. AIR FRIED SAUSAGE WITH BELL PEPPER 17

   15. AIR FRYER LEMON PEPPER SHRIMP 18

   16. AIR FRYER BRUSSELS SPROUTS 18

   17. AIR FRYER CHICKEN MILANESE WITH ARUGULA 19

   18. AIR FRYER BASIL-PARMESAN SALMON 20

   19. AIR FRYER GARLICAND PARSLEY BABY POTATOES 21

   20. AIR FRYER CRISPY BREADED PORK CHOPS 21

   21. AIR FRYER ZUCCHINI TURKEY BURGERS 22

   22. AIR FRYER BACON WRAPPED CHICKEN BITES 23

   23. AIR FRYER CHEESEBURGERS 24

   24. AIR FRYER MOZZARELLA STICKS 25

   25. AIR FRYER BEEF EMPANADAS 26

   26. AIR FRYER CINNAMON APPLE CHIPS 26

   27. CRISPY AVOCADO FRIES 27

   28. AIR FRIED SHISHITO PEPPERS 28

29. Air Fryer Salmon with Maple Soy Glaze and Garlic 28
30. Parmesan Fried Tortellini 29
31. Garlic Parmesan Chicken 30
32. Air Fried Sweet Potato Hash 31
33. Air Fryer Cinnamon and Sugar Doughnuts 31
34. Air Fryer Garlicand Parsley Baby Potatoes 32
35. Air Fried Hot Dogs 33
36. Air Fried Avocado Egg Rolls 34
37. Air Fried Crumbed Chicken Tenderloins 35
38. Air Fried Ribeye Steak 35
39. Fried Asparagus with Spicy Mayo Dip 36
40. Air Fryer Zucchini Chips 38
41. Air Fried Coconut Shrimp 38
42. Air Fried Corn on the Cob 39
43. Air-Fried Butter Cake 40
44. Air Fryer Beef Satay 40
45. Keto Air Fried Chicken Meatballs 41
46. Air-Fryer Roasted Veggies 42
47. Air Fryer Steak with Garlic Herb Butter 43
48. Air Fryer Eggplant Parmesan 44
49. Low Carb Air Fried Onion Rings 45
50. Air Fryer French Toast Sticks 45
51. Fryer Sausage Patties 46
52. Air Fried Buffalo Cauliflower Bites 47
53. Air Fryer Fish and Chips 47
54. Air Fried Okra 48
55. Air Fryer Chicken Wings 49
56. Air Fryer Sweet Potato Tots 50
57. Air Fryer Coconut Pie Recipe (Gluten-Free) 50
58. Air Fried Bacon and Cream Cheese Stuffed Jalapeno Poppers 51
59. Cilantro Ranch Sweet Potato Cauliflower Patties 52
60. Keto Air Fryer Shrimp Scampi 53
61. Air Fried Chicken Nuggets Recipe 54
62. Air Fryer Chips 55
63. Air Fried Walnuts Loaf Recipe 55

- 64. Air Fryer Bacon 56
- 65. Air Fried Salmon 57
- 66. Air Fryer Mexican Street Corn Recipe 57
- 67. Air Fryer Chicken Sandwich 58
- 68. Air Fryer Chicken Burritos 59
- 69. Air Fryer Nachos 60
- 70. Air Fryer Fried Catfish Recipe 61
- 71. Air Fried Ham & Egg Toast Cup 61
- 72. Air fryer Beetroot Chips 62
- 73. Air Fried Coconut Shrimp with Marmalade Sauce 63
- 74. Air Fryer Spicy Chicken Thighs 64
- 75. Gluten-free Air Fried Jalapeno Poppers 65
- 76. Air Fried Fish Finger Sandwich 66
- 77. Air Fried Taco Bell Crunch Wrap 67
- 78. Air Fryer Roasted Black pepper Pork Ribs 68
- 79. Air Fried Bow Tie Pasta Chips 68
- 80. Air Fried Sweet-Sour Pork 69
- 81. Air Fryer Vegan Stuffed Potatoes 70
- 82. Air Fried Tofu Rancheros 71
- 83. Air Fried Eggless Chocolate Chip Muffins 72
- 84. Vegan Air Fried Carrot Cake 73
- 85. Air Fried Blueberriesand Apple Crumble 74
- 86. Air Fried Seitan Vegan Riblets with Mushroom 75
- 87. Air Fried Pecan-Crusted Gardein Fishless Filets 76
- 88. Air Fryer Tofu with Orange Sauce 76
- 89. Air Fryer Caribbean Spiced Chicken 77
- 90. Air Fried Sriracha Honey Chicken Wings 78
- 91. Coconut Shrimp with Marmalade Sauce 79
- 92. Air fryer french fries 80
- 93. Air Fryer Cauliflower Chickpea Tacos 80
- 94. Air Fryer Coconut Shrimp With Pina Colada Dip 81
- 95. Air Fried Fish Sticks with Tartar Sauce 82
- 96. Air Fried Thai Salmon Patties 83
- 97. Air Fryer Carrot Mug Cake 84
- 98. Air Fried Brownies 85

99. AIR FRIED TURKEY BREAST WITH CHERRY GLAZE ... 86
100. AIR FRYER BUFFALO CAULIFLOWER ... 87
101. AIR FRIED KALE CHIPS ... 87
102. AIR FRYER TURKEY FAJITAS PLATTER ... 88
103. AIR FRIED SWEET POTATO CAULIFLOWER PATTIES WITH RANCH ... 89
104. AIR FRIED SPRING ROLLS WITH SWEET SOUR SAUCE ... 90
105. TWICE AIR-FRIED VEGAN STUFFED POTATOES WITH KALE ... 91
106. AIR FRIED CRISPY ASIAN BROCCOLI ... 92
107. AIR FRIED JALAPENO POPPER STUFFED CHICKEN RECIPE ... 93
108. AIR FRIED CHICKEN WINGS WITH HONEY AND SRIRACHA SAUCE ... 94
109. AIR FRYER CARIBBEAN SPICED CHICKEN ... 95
110. AIR FRYER ROASTED CHICKPEAS RECIPE ... 96
111. AIR FRIED MEATLOAF RECIPE ... 96
112. AIR FRIED SESAME GINGER CARROTS WITH SCALLIONS ... 97
113. AIR FRIED CHINESE SALT AND PEPPER PORK CHOPS RECIPE ... 98
114. THAI FISH CAKES WITH MANGO SALSA ... 99
115. AIR FRYER BAKED GARLIC PARSLEY POTATOES ... 100
116. AIR FRIED CILANTRO LIME SHRIMP SKEWERS ... 101
117. AIR FRYER SMOKED RIBS ... 102
118. VEGAN AIR FRYER CRISPY CHICKPEA TACOS ... 102
119. KETO AIR FRYER HARD BOILED EGGS RECIPE ... 103
120. GLUTEN-FREE AIR FRYER STEAK WITH HERB LEMON BUTTER ... 104
121. AIR FRIED CHOCOLATE CHIP ZUCCHINI BREAD ... 105
122. AIR FRIED BUFFALO CAULIFLOWER WINGS ... 106
123. AIR FRIED PLANTAINS ... 106
124. AIR FRIED TATER TOTS RECIPE ... 107
125. AIR FRIED ROSEMARY TURKEY BREAST WITH MAPLE MUSTARD GLAZE ... 108
126. AIR FRIED LEMON GREEN BEANS ... 109
127. AIR FRIED MINI NUTELLA APPLE PIES ... 110
128. AIR FRIED TOMATO AND ONION QUICHE ... 111
129. AIR FRYER CAULIFLOWER TATER TOTS ... 112
130. AIR FRIED RICE WITH SESAME AND SRIRACHA SAUCE ... 113
131. AIR FRYER MINI SWEDISH MEATBALLS ... 114
132. AIR FRIED BANANA BREAD ... 115
133. AIR FRIED LAMB RACK WITH MACADAMIA ROSEMARY CRUST ... 116

134. Air Fryer Roasted Paprika Potatoes with Greek Yoghurt	117
135. Air Fryer Stuffed Portobello Mushrooms	118
136. Air Fryer Cheese Loaf Recipe	119
137. Air Fried Fish and Chips Recipe	120
138. Air Fryer Fried Pickles with Italian Seasoning	121
139. Air Fryer Roast Chicken with Rosemary	122
140. Air Fried Spicy Drumsticks with Barbecue Marinade	123
141. Air Fried Bread Recipe	124
142. Air Fried Prawns with Cocktail Sauce	125
143. Air Fried Ricotta Balls with Chives	126
144. Air Fried Puff Pastry Bites Recipe	127
145. Air Fried Basil-Parmesan Salmon Recipe	128
146. Air Fried Chicken Chimichanga Recipe	128
147. Air Fried Apricot and Blackberry Crumble Recipe	130
148. Air Fryer Mushroom Croquettes Recipe	131
149. Air Fried Potato Croquettes with Parmesan Cheese Recipe	132
150. Air Fried Asian-Glazed Boneless Chicken Thighs Recipe	133
151. Air fried Stuffed Bagel Recipe	134
152. Air Fried Parmesan Garlic Knots with Parsley	135
153. Air Fried Buffalo Chicken Egg Rolls Recipe	136
154. Air Fried Cauliflower Rice Balls Recipe	137
155. Air Fried Mascarpone Mushroom Pasta Recipe	138
156. Air Fried Cilantro Pesto Chicken Legs with Lemon	139
157. Air Fried Spicy Lamb Sirloin Steak Recipe	140
158. Keto Air Fried Lasagna Recipe	141
159. Air Fried Taco Meatballs Recipe	142
160. Air Fried Chicken Jalfrezi Recipe	143
161. Keto Air Fried Salmon Vegetables Recipe	144
162. Air Fried Korean Chicken Wings with Gochujang & Mayonnaise Dressing	145
163. Air Fried Scotch Eggs with Pepper Sauce Recipe	146
164. Air Fried Chicken with Indian Fennel Recipe	147
165. Air Fried Pork Chops with Vietnamese Thit Nuong	148
166. Air Fried Brazilian Tempero Baino Chicken Drumsticks	149
167. Air Fried Cornish Game Hens Recipe	150
168. Air Fried Mini Quiche Wedges with Mushroom	151

169. AIR FRIED BROWN NUT LOAF RECIPE 152
170. AIR FRIED BEEF RIB CROQUETTES 152
171. AIR FRIED SALMON SPRING ONION CROQUETTES WITH GARLIC 153
172. AIR FRIED ROASTED CHICKEN WITH BUTTERMILK MARINADE 154
173. AIR FIED TWICE FRIED PLANTAINS 155
174. AIR FRIED HAM-KING PRAWNS WITH RED PEPPER DIP AND PAPRIKA 156
175. AIR FRIED CINNAMON ROLLED MEAT 157
176. AIR FRIED LAMB LOIN CHOPS WITH ZA'ATAR 158
177. AIR FRIED TURKISH CHICKEN RECIPE 158
178. AIR FRIED BUTTERED-SHRIMP WITH CHICKEN STOCK 159
179. AIR FRIED SCALLOPS WITH BASIL 160
180. AIR FRYER HERBED TANDOORI CHICKEN 161
181. AIR FRIED CHICKEN COCONUT MEATBALLS RECIPE 162
182. AIR FRIED SALAD WITH GREEK YOGHURT & ROASTED PEPPER DRESSING 163
183. AIR FRIED MINI FRANKFURTERS PASTRY WITH MUSTARD 164
184. AIR FRYER ZUCCHINI TURKEY BURGERS RECIPE 164
185. AIR FRYER AVOCADO FRIES WITH LIME SAUCE 165
186. AIR FRIED LAMB MEATBALLS WITH LEMON PEEL & GREEK FETA 166
187. AIR FRIED CRISPY BACON WRAPPED SCALLOPS 167
188. AIR FRIED BEEF BULGOGI BURGERS WITH SCALLIONS & GOCHUJANG 167
189. AIR FRYER PARMESAN SCOTCH EGGS 168
190. AIR FRIED ROASTED ASPARAGUS AND AVOCADO SOUP RECIPE 169
191. VEGAN AIR FRIED ROASTED GARLIC RECIPE 170
192. AIR FRYER BROWN LOAF WITH SUNFLOWER SEEDS 171
193. AIR FRYER RATATOUILLE RECIPE 171
194. AIR FRIED ROASTED OREGANO PEPPER ROLLS WITH FETA CHEESE 172
195. AIR FRYER CRISPY ROASTED ONION POTATOES 173
196. AIR FRIED CHOCOLATE CAKE WITH COCOA POWDER 174
197. AIR FRIED FETA TRIANGLES WITH GREEN ONION RECIPE 175
198. KETO AIR FRIED MEATLOAF SLIDERS RECIPE 176
199. VEGAN AIR FRIED CRISPY RAVIOLI RECIPE 177
200. AIR FRIED BRATWURST WITH CRUSTY BREAD ROLLS RECIPE 178

CONCLUSION 179

INTRODUCTION

Air frying, generally referred to as hot air frying, is a modern cooking technique which has been developed to allow for the frying, roasting or grilling of food without using the copious oil or fat amounts we are used to. How does it taste without generous use of oil? The truth is the technology ensures that the food being prepared gets not only the taste of deep fried food but also the texture. Grease is one of the major causes of cardiovascular diseases and if you are able to eliminate it from your diet, then you are safer from these conditions more than never before.

Since the acquisition of the microwaves and the slow cookers around the 1970s, no other kitchen acquisition surpasses the innovation of the hot air frying machines. The appliances have a design that allows for the circulation of extremely hot air in such a fashion mimicking the flow and movement of heat currents within a pot with boiling oil. This thus enables the system to crisp the outside of the food whereas the inside is allowed to cook. Some modernized designs come with grilling elements that are essential for added crispness and browning.

In a nutshell, the air frying system in conjunction with the air fryer has been designed to be used for oil-less healthy cooking. The result is food that is very moist and well-cooked on the inside with the outside being crispy, brown and very appealing to the eye.

An air fryer can be used to cook different meals such as French fries, tater tots, onion rings, homemade potato chips, baked potatoes, grilled cheese sandwiches, roasted vegetables, corn on the cob, empanadas, egg rolls, spring rolls, crab Rangoon, donut, chicken, hamburgers, bacon, fish, and more.

You can use an air fryer to make your favorite meals just as the regular deep-fried, sautéed, grilled, and baked meals. An air fryer requires only a little oil and hot air to fry your meals.

Benefits of Using This Air Fryer Cookbook!

There are several new gadgets coming in the market each and every day to make sure the flexible life. Air fryer is on of them which has made a great change showing few exclusive features in cooking. Now we will know few real benefits of using air fryer which can make a significant change in cooking.

A. Produces a better frying result:

First of all, your favorite foods will be back on the menu: One reason why you have been advised not to eat most of the junk foods is not because of their primary composition but because of what they result in after preparation. Upon frying with an air fryer, nutritionists will approve the same food that they advised you not to eat.

B. Makes use of natural healthy oil:

The natural healthy fats and oils are ideal for this frying. If you want an oily taste and appearance, you can stuff your food with walnut oil, avocado oil, grape seed oil among others. There is no limit as far as healthy gourmet cooking oils for hot air frying are concerned.

C. Reduces the hassle that is associated with the regular frying version:

As mentioned earlier, the hassles that come with deep frying are highly reduced or completely eliminated in some aspects when this method is employed.

D. Air frying is economic:

Cooking oils and fats cost you much, especially where deep frying is involved. Imagine a case where you enjoy sweet food yet you end up saving all that which you would have spent on cooking oil.

E. Speed of Cooking :

The air fryer's small convection oven preheats and cooks more quickly than a conventional oven. You'll have tasty meals in haste, with less waiting time! Some recipes take 20-50 % less time in an air fryer.

F. Simple and Easy :

Air fryers utilize simple controls, typically two knobs for cook time and temperature, or an easy to read digital display. You simply toss the food in oil (if desired), place it in the basket, and the air fryer does the rest.

G. Safe :

Lacking the large oil vats of traditional deep fryers, air fryers eliminate the risk of serious burns from spilled oil. Also, air fryers are designed so that the exterior does not become dangerously hot to the touch.

An air fryer can prepare foods that would normally go in a deep fryer. Spraying foods like fries or onion rings with oil allows the intense circulating heat of the machine to cook a crisp exterior and tender interior. Most recipes only call for about 1 tablespoon of oil, which is best applied with a mister.

Fatty foods, like bacon, won't need you to add any oil. Leaner meats, however, will need some oiling to keep them from sticking to the pan.

Why Are You Use This Air Fryer Cookbook?

There are a number a reasons why using this book will be beneficial to you.

One reason is that this ebook gives you a wide array of recipes to choose from, hence you are not limited in terms of choice. The ebook contains healthy recipes that are easy to cook in your air fryer gadget.

With this book, you needn't worry about your dietry restrictions as there are many recipes adapted to suit your specific needs. You are going to find vegan recipes, keto recipes, lowcarb recipes, and even pasta.

Also noteworthy is the fact that this ebook provides you with just the best alternative to the traditional deep frying version.

You will learn how to grill, bake, saute, roast and fry your favorite meals with air fryer.

This ebook examines some recipes that you will enjoy cooking in an air fryer.

Let's now examine 200 different recipes that you will enjoy cooking in your air fryer gadget. Are you thinking about your dietary restrictions? Don't worry about any dietary restrictions you may have. There are plenty of great recipes here that cater to your specific needs!

EASY AIR FRYER RECIPES THAT CATER TO YOUR SPECIFIC NEEDS

Air Fried Pork Taquitos

Prep Time: 15 mins; Cook Time: 12 mins; Total Time: 27 mins.

Yield: 5 Servings.

INGREDIENTS
- 3 cups cooked shredded pork tenderloin
- 2 1/2 cups fat-free shredded mozzarella
- 10 small flour tortillas
- 1 lime, juiced

INSTRUCTIONS
1. Preheat air fryer to 3750F.
2. Sprinkle lime juice over pork and gently mix around.
3. Microwave 5 tortillas at a time with a damp paper towel over it for 10 seconds, to soften.
4. Add 3 ounces of pork and 1/4 cup of cheese to a tortilla.
5. Tightly and gently roll up the tortillas.
6. Line tortillas on a greased foil-lined pan.
7. Spray an even coat of cooking spray over tortillas.
8. Air Fry for 10 minutes until tortillas are a golden color, flipping halfway through.
9. When done cooking, remove from air fryer and serve.

NUTRITIONAL FACTS (Per Serving)
- **256 calories; 4g fat; 31.2g protein; 19g net carbs.**

Air Fryer Breakfast Frittata

Prep Time: 15 mins; Cook Time: 20 mins; Total Time: 35 mins.

Yield: 2 Servings.

INGREDIENTS
- 1/4 pound breakfast sausage, fully cooked and crumbled
- Cooking spray
- 4 eggs, lightly beaten
- 1/2 cup shredded cheese
- 2 tablespoons red bell pepper, diced
- 1 green onion, chopped
- 1 pinch cayenne pepper (optional)

INSTRUCTIONS
1. Place sausage, eggs, and cheese in a mixing bowl and mix. Add bell pepper, onion, and cayenne and mix well to combine.
2. Preheat the air fryer to 360 F.
3. Spray a nonstick 6x2-inch cake pan with cooking spray.
4. Place egg mixture in the prepared cake pan.
5. Cook in the air fryer for about 20 minutes or until frittata is set.
6. Serve and enjoy.

NUTRITIONAL FACTS (Per Serving)
- **380 calories; 27g fat; 3g carbs; 31g protein.**

CINNAMONROLLS

Prep Time: 20 mins; Cook Time: 20 mins; Total Time: 40 mins.

Yield: 8 Rolls.

INGREDIENTS
- 1 pound frozen bread dough, thawed
- ¼ cup butter, melted and cooled
- ¾ cup brown sugar
- 1½ tablespoons ground cinnamon,

Cream Cheese Glaze
- ❖ 4 ounces cream cheese, softened
- ❖ 2 tablespoons butter, softened
- ❖ 1¼ cups powdered sugar
- ❖ ½ teaspoon vanilla

INSTRUCTIONS

1. Let the bread dough come to room temperature on the counter. On a lightly floured surface roll the dough into a 13-inch by 11-inch rectangle. Position the rectangle so the 13-inch side is facing you. Brush the melted butter all over the dough, leaving a 1-inch border uncovered along the edge farthest away from you.
2. Combine the brown sugar and cinnamon in a small bowl. Sprinkle the mixture evenly over the buttered dough, keeping the 1-inch border uncovered. Roll the dough into a log starting with the edge closest to you. Roll the dough tightly, making sure to roll evenly and push out any air pockets. When you get to the uncovered edge of the dough, press the dough onto the roll to seal it together.
3. Cut the log into 8 pieces, slicing slowly with a sawing motion so you don't flatten the dough. Turn the slices on their sides and cover with a clean kitchen towel. Let the rolls sit in the warmest part of your kitchen for 1½ to hours to rise.
4. Meanwhile, make the glaze. Place the cream cheese and butter in a microwave-safe bowl. Soften the mixture in the microwave for 30 seconds at a time until it is easy to stir. Gradually add the powdered sugar and stir to combine.
5. Add the vanilla extract and whisk until smooth. Set aside. When the rolls have risen, pre-heat the air fryer to 350°F.
6. Transfer 4 of the rolls to the air fryer basket. Air-fry for 5 minutes. Turn the rolls over and air-fry for another 4 minutes. Repeat with the remaining 4 rolls. Let the rolls cool for a couple of minutes before glazing.
7. Spread large dollops of cream cheese glaze on top of the warm cinnamon rolls, allowing some of the glaze to drip down the side of the rolls. Serve warm and enjoy!

NUTRITIONAL FACTS (Per Serving)

✓ **470 Calories;19g Fat;17g Net Carbs;7g Protein.**

Crispy Avocado Fries

Prep Time: 5 mins; Cook Time: 10 mins; Total Time: 15 mins.

Yields: 4 servings.

INGREDIENTS
- 1 cup Panko breadcrumbs
- 1 teaspoon garlic powder
- 1 teaspoon paprika
- 1 cup all-purpose flour
- 2 large eggs
- 2 avocados, sliced
- Ranch, for serving (optional)

INSTRUCTIONS
1. In a shallow bowl, whisk together Panko, garlic powder, and paprika. Place flour in another shallow bowl, and in a third shallow bowl beat eggs.
2. One at a time, dip avocado slices into flour, then egg, then Panko mixture until fully coated.
3. Place in an air fryer and fry at 400° for 10 minutes.
4. Serve with ranch (if using).

NUTRITIONAL FACTS (Per Serving)
- **262 calories; 18g fat; 16g net carbs; 5g protein.**

Air Fryer Banana Bread

Prep Time: 10 mins; Cook Time: 35 mins; Total Time: 45 Mins.

Yield: 8 Servings.

INGREDIENTS
- 2 medium ripe bananas, mashed
- 2 large eggs, lightly beaten
- 3/4 cup white-whole wheat flour
- 1 teaspoon cinnamon
- 1/2 teaspoon Kosher salt
- 1/4 teaspoon Baking soda
- 1/2 cup granulated sugar

- ❖ 1/3 cup plain nonfat yogurt
- ❖ 2 tablespoons vegetable oil
- ❖ 1 teaspoon Vanilla extract
- ❖ 2 tablespoons toasted walnuts, roughly chopped
- ❖ Cooking spray

INSTRUCTIONS

1. Line the bottom of a 6-inch round cake pan with parchment paper; lightly coat pan with cooking spray. Whisk together flour, cinnamon, salt and baking soda in a medium bowl; set aside.
2. In a separate medium bowl, whisk together mashed bananas, eggs, sugar, yogurt, oil, and vanilla. Gently stir wet ingredients into flour mixture until well combined. Pour batter into prepared pan and sprinkle with walnuts.
3. Heat a 5.3-qt air fryer to 310°F and then place the pan in the air fryer and cook until browned and a wooden pick inserted in the middle comes out clean, about 35 minutes, turning the pan halfway while cooking.
4. Transfer bread to a wire rack to cool in the pan for 15 minutes before turning out and slicing.
5. Serve and enjoy!

NUTRITIONAL FACTS (Per Serving)

- ✓ 184 calories; 29g carbs; 1g fiber; 16g sugars; 6g fat; 4g protein.

Churros with Chocolate Sauce

Prep Time:20 mins; Cook Time: 50 mins;

Total Time: 1 hour 10 mins.

Yield: 12 Churros (2 churros + 2 teaspoons chocolate sauce = 1 serve)

INGREDIENTS

- ❖ 1/2 cup water
- ❖ 1/4 teaspoon kosher salt
- ❖ 1/4 cup plus 2 tablespoons unsalted butter, divided
- ❖ 1/2 cup all-purpose flour
- ❖ 2 large eggs
- ❖ 2 tablespoons vanilla kefir
- ❖ 1/3 cup granulated sugar

- ❖ 2 teaspoons ground cinnamon
- ❖ 4 ounces bittersweet baking chocolate, finely chopped
- ❖ 3 tablespoons heavy cream

INSTRUCTIONS

1. Place water in a small saucepan over medium-high, add salt and 1/4 cup of the butter and bring to a boil.
2. Reduce heat to medium-low; add flour, and stir vigorously with a wooden spoon until dough is smooth, about 30 seconds. Continue cooking, stirring constantly, until dough begins to pull away from sides of the pan and a film forms on bottom of the pan, 3 minutes.
3. Transfer dough to a medium bowl. Stir constantly until slightly cooled, about 1 minute.
4. Add eggs, 1 at a time, stirring constantly until completely smooth after each addition.
5. Transfer mixture to a piping bag fitted with a medium star tip. Chill for 30 minutes.
6. Pipe 6 (3-inch long) pieces in a single layer in the air fryer basket. Cook at 380°F until golden, about 10 minutes. Repeat with remaining dough.
7. Stir together sugar and cinnamon in a medium bowl. Brush cooked churros with remaining 2 tablespoons melted butter, and roll in sugar mixture to coat.
8. Place chocolate and cream in a small microwavable bowl.
9. Microwave on high until melted and smooth, about 30 seconds, stirring after 15 seconds.
10. Add kefir and stir. Serve churros with chocolate sauce.

NUTRITIONAL FACTS (Per Serving)

✓ **253 calories; 14.4g fat; 20g carbs; 2g fiber; 5g protein.**

Air-Fried Cinnamon Apple Chips with Almond Yogurt Dip

Prep Time: 10 mins; Cook Time: 15 mins;Total Time: 25 mins.
Yield: 4 Servings.

INGREDIENTS

- ❖ 1 (8-oz.) apple
- ❖ 1 teaspoon ground cinnamon

- ❖ 2 teaspoons canola oil
- ❖ Cooking spray
- ❖ 1/4 cup plain 1% low-fat Greek yogurt
- ❖ 1 tablespoon almond butter
- ❖ 1 teaspoon honey

INSTRUCTIONS

1. Thinly slice apple on a mandoline. Place slices in a bowl with cinnamon and oil; toss to coat evenly.
2. Coat air fryer basket well with cooking spray. Place 7 to 8 apple slices in a single layer in your air fryer basket, and cook at 375°F for 12 minutes, turning the slices every 4 minutes and rearranging slices to flatten them, as they will move during the cooking process. Repeat with remaining apple slices.
3. While apple slices cook, stir together yogurt, almond butter, and honey in a small bowl until smooth. To serve, place 6 to 8 apple slices on each plate with a small dollop of dipping sauce. Enjoy!

NUTRITIONAL FACTS (Per Serving)

- ✓ 104 calories; 3g fat; 14g net carbs, 1g protein.

Bourbon Bacon Burger

Prep Time: 10 mins; Cook Time: 25 mins; Total Time: 35 mins.

Yield: 2 Servings.

INGREDIENTS

For the Burger

- ❖ 3/4 pound ground beef 80% lean
- ❖ 1 tablespoon minced onion
- ❖ 2 tablespoons BBQ sauce
- ❖ 1/2 teaspoon salt
- ❖ 2 Kaiser rolls
- ❖ freshly ground black pepper, to taste

For the Burger Sauce

- ❖ 2 tablespoons BBQ sauce
- ❖ 2 tablespoons mayonnaise
- ❖ 1/4 teaspoon ground paprika
- ❖ freshly ground black pepper, to taste

Toppings
- ❖ 2 slices Monterey Jack cheese
- ❖ lettuce
- ❖ tomato
- ❖ 1 tablespoon bourbon
- ❖ 2 tablespoons brown sugar
- ❖ 3 strips maple bacon, cut in half

INSTRUCTIONS

1. Preheat the air fryer to 390°F and pour a little water into the bottom of the air fryer drawer.
2. Combine the bourbon and brown sugar in a small bowl. Place the bacon strips in the air fryer basket and brush with the brown sugar mixture. Air-fry at 390°F for 4 minutes.
3. Flip the bacon over, brush with more brown sugar and air-fry at 390°F for another 4 minutes until crispy.
4. While the bacon is cooking, make the burger patties. Combine the ground beef, onion, BBQ sauce, salt and pepper in a large bowl. Mix well with your hands until combined and shape the meat into 2 patties.
5. Transfer the burger patties to the air fryer basket and air-fry the burgers at 370°F for 15 minutes, or until cooked through. Flip the burgers over halfway through the cooking process.
6. Meanwhile, make the burger sauce by combining the BBQ sauce, mayonnaise, paprika, and freshly ground black pepper to taste in a bowl.
7. When the burgers are cooked to your liking, top each patty with a slice of Monterey Jack cheese and air-fry for an additional minute, just to melt the cheese.
8. You might want to pin the cheese slice to the burger with a toothpick to prevent it from blowing off in your air fryer.
9. Spread the sauce on the inside of the Kaiser rolls, place the burgers on the rolls, top with the bourbon bacon, lettuce, and tomato.
10. Enjoy!

NUTRITIONAL FACTS (Per Serving)

- ✓ **240 calories; 10g net carbs; 14g fat; 16g protein.**

Air Fried Sweet Potato Dessert Fries

Prep Time: 5 mins; Cook Time: 20 mins; Total Time: 25 mins.

Yield: 4 Servings.

INGREDIENTS

- 2 medium sweet potatoes
- Half a tablespoon of coconut oil.
- 1 tablespoon arrowroot starch
- 2 teaspoons melted butter, Optional
- 1/4 cup coconut sugar
- 2 tablespoons cinnamon
- Powdered sugar for dusting, Optional

Dipping Sauces

- Dessert Hummus
- Vanilla Greek Yogurt
- Maple Frosting

INSTRUCTIONS

1. Peel your sweet potatoes and wash them with clean water, then dry.
2. Slice peeled sweet potatoes lengthwise, 1/2 inch thick.
3. Toss your sweet potato slices in 1/2 tablespoon coconut oil and arrowroot starch
4. Place in an air fryer for 18 minutes at 370F. Shake halfway while it's cooking.
5. Remove the fries from the air fryer and place in a large bowl. Drizzle butter on top of fries. Then mix in cinnamon and sugar and toss fries together again.
6. Place on serving plate and sprinkle with powdered sugar
7. Serve fries with a dipping sauce of choice.

NUTRITIONAL FACTS (Per Serving)

- 130 calories; 23g fat; 23.9g net carbs; 1.2g protein.

Zesty Ranch Air Fryer Fish Fillets

Prep Time: 6 mins; Cook Time: 12 mins;Total Time: 18 mins.

Yield: 4 Servings.

INGREDIENTS
- 3/4 cup bread crumbs
- 1 30g packet dry ranch-style dressing mix
- 2 1/2 tablespoons vegetable oil
- 2 eggs beaten
- 4 tilapia salmon or other fish fillets
- lemon wedges for garnish

INSTRUCTIONS
1. Preheat your air fryer to 3560F.
2. Mix the breadcrumbs and the ranch dressing mix together. Add in the oil and keep stirring until the mixture becomes loose and crumbly.
3. Dip the fish fillets into the egg, letting the excess drip off.
4. Dip the fish fillets into the crumb mixture, making sure to coat them evenly and thoroughly.
5. Place into your air fryer carefully.
6. Cook for 12 minutes.
7. Remove and serve. Squeeze the lemon wedges over the fish if desired.

NUTRITIONAL FACTS (Per Serving)
- ✓ 315 calories; 8g carbs; 38g protein; 14g fat.

Air Fryer Raspberry Balsamic Smoked Pork Chops

Prep: 15 mins; Cook: 15 mins;Total Time: 30 mins.

Yield: 4 Servings (1 pork chop+1 tablespoon glaze = 1 serve)

INGREDIENTS
- 2 large eggs
- 2 tablespoons brown sugar
- 1 cup panko bread crumbs
- 1 cup finely chopped pecans
- 4 smoked bone-in pork chops (7 1/2 ounces each)

- 1/4 cup all-purpose flour
- 1/4 cup 2% milk
- 1/3 cup balsamic vinegar
- 2 tablespoons seedless raspberry jam
- 1 tablespoon thawed frozen orange juice concentrate

INSTRUCTIONS

1. Preheat air fryer to 400°. Spray air fryer basket with cooking spray. In a shallow bowl, whisk together eggs and milk. In another shallow bowl, toss bread crumbs with pecans.
2. Coat pork chops with flour; shake off excess. Dip in egg mixture, then in crumb mixture, patting to help adhere. Working in batches as needed, place chops in a single layer in air fryer basket; spritz with cooking spray.
3. Cook until golden brown, 15 minutes, turning halfway through cooking and spritzing with additional cooking spray. Remove and keep warm. Repeat with remaining chops.
4. Meanwhile, place the remaining ingredients in a small saucepan; bring to a boil. Cook and stir until slightly thickened, 6 minutes. Serve.

NUTRITIONAL FACTS (Per Serving)

- 579 calories; 36g fat; 33g net carbs; 32g protein.

Air Fryer Coconut Shrimp with Piña Colada Dip

Prep Time: 15 mins; Cook Time: 10 mins;Total Time: 25 mins.

Yield: About 20 Shrimps.

INGREDIENTS

For the shrimp

- 1 1/2 pounds jumbo shrimp
- 2/3 cup light coconut milk
- 2 tablespoons honey
- 1 cup unsweetened shredded coconut
- 1/2 cup cornstarch
- 3/4 cup panko bread crumbs

For the sauce

- 1/3 cup light coconut milk
- 1/3 cup plain nonfat Greek yogurt
- 1/4 cup pineapple chunks drained
- 1/4 teaspoon salt more to taste
- 1/4 teaspoon pepper more to taste
- Toasted coconut for garnish

INSTRUCTIONS

1. Remove the shell from the shrimp, leaving the tail intact, if desired.
2. Place cornstarch in a gallon-size bag and add the shrimp. Toss to coat.
3. In a medium bowl, whisk coconut milk and honey until combined. In another medium bowl, combine coconut and panko. Remove shrimp from the bag, gently knocking off any excess cornstarch. Dunk shrimp in the liquid mixture, then dredge in the coconut mixture. You may have to press loose coconut and panko gently onto the shrimp.
4. Transfer coated shrimp to the basket of your air fryer.
5. Heat your fryer to 3500F and cook 6-8 minutes, flipping shrimp once, until the coconut is golden brown and the shrimp are cooked through.
6. Meanwhile, prepare the sauce. In a medium bowl, combine coconut milk, yogurt, pineapple, salt, and pepper in a bowl. Top with toasted coconut.
7. Serve and enjoy!

NUTRITIONAL FACTS (Per Serving)

- ✓ **186 calories; 24g carbs; 19g sugars; 10g fat; 2g protein.**

Air-Fryer-Garlic-Rosemary Brussels Sprouts

Prep Time: 12 mins; Cook Time: 18 mins;Total Time: 30 mins.

Yield: 4 Servings (serving size: 3/4 cup).

INGREDIENTS

- 1 pound Brussels sprouts, trimmed and halved
- 1 1/2 teaspoons minced fresh rosemary
- 3 tablespoons olive oil
- 2 garlic cloves, minced
- 1/2 teaspoon salt

- ❖ 1/4 teaspoon pepper
- ❖ 1/2 cup panko bread crumbs

INSTRUCTIONS

1. Preheat air fryer to 350°F. Place the olive in a small microwave-safe bowl add garlic, salt, and pepper. Microwave on high for 30 seconds.
2. Toss Brussels sprouts with 2 tablespoons oil mixture. Place all the Brussels sprouts in the fryer basket and cook 5 minutes.
3. Stir sprouts. Continue to air-fry until sprouts are lightly browned and near desired tenderness, about 8 minutes longer, stirring halfway through cooking time.
4. Toss bread crumbs with rosemary and remaining oil mixture; sprinkle over sprouts. Continue cooking for about 4 minutes until crumbs are browned and sprouts are tender.
5. Serve immediately.

NUTRITIONAL FACTS (Per Serving)

✓ 164 calories; 11g fat; 11g net carbs; 5g protein.

Air Fried Sausage with Bell Pepper

**Prep Time: 15 mins; Cook Time: 20 mins;Total Time: 35 mins.
Yield: 2 Servings.**

INGREDIENTS

- ❖ 1/4 pound breakfast sausage, fully cooked and crumbled
- ❖ 1/2 cup shredded cheddar cheese blend
- ❖ 2 tablespoons red bell pepper, diced
- ❖ 1 green onion, chopped
- ❖ 4 eggs, lightly beaten
- ❖ cooking spray
- ❖ 1 pinch cayenne pepper, optional

INSTRUCTIONS

1. Combine sausage, eggs, cheese, bell pepper, onion, and cayenne in a bowl and mix to combine.
2. Preheat the air fryer to 375 f.
3. Spray a nonstick 6x2-inch cake pan with cooking spray.
4. Place egg mixture in the prepared cake pan.
5. Cook in the air fryer for about 20 minutes or until frittata is set.

NUTRITIONAL FACTS (Per Serving)
- ✓ 380 calories; 27.4 g fat; 2.9 g net carbs; 31.2 g protein.

Air Fryer Lemon Pepper Shrimp

Prep Time: 5 mins; Cook Time: 10 mins;Total Time: 15 mins.

Yield: 2 servings.

INGREDIENTS
- ❖ 12 ounces uncooked medium shrimp, peeled and deveined
- ❖ 1 lemon, juiced
- ❖ 1 tablespoon olive oil
- ❖ 1 teaspoon lemon pepper
- ❖ 1/4 teaspoon paprika
- ❖ 1/4 teaspoon garlic powder

INSTRUCTIONS
1. Preheat an air fryer to 400 F.
2. Combine olive oil, lemon juice, lemon pepper, paprika, and garlic powder in a bowl. Add shrimp and toss until coated.
3. Place shrimp in the air fryer and cook for 8 minutes or until pink and firm.
4. Serve garnished with lemon slices.

NUTRITIONAL FACTS (Per Serving)
- ✓ **215 calories; 8.6 g fat; 7 g net carbohydrates; 28.9 g protein; 5.5g fiber.**

Air Fryer Brussels Sprouts

Prep Time: 5 mins; Cook Time: 10 mins;Total Time: 15 mins.

Yield: 2 Servings.

INGREDIENTS
- ❖ 10 ounces Brussels sprouts, trimmed and halved lengthwise
- ❖ 1 teaspoon avocado oil
- ❖ 1 teaspoon balsamic vinegar
- ❖ 2 teaspoons cooked bacon, crumbled (optional)
- ❖ 1/2 teaspoon salt
- ❖ Fresh ground black pepper to taste

INSTRUCTIONS

1. Preheat an air fryer to 350 F.
2. In mixing bowl, combine oil, salt, and pepper. Mix well to combine.
3. Add Brussels sprouts and turn to coat.
4. Air fry for 5 minutes, shake the sprouts and cook for another 5 minutes.
5. Transfer sprouts to a serving dish, sprinkle with balsamic vinegar and turn to coat.
6. Top with crumbled bacon.
7. Serve and enjoy!

NUTRITIONAL FACTS (Per Serving)

- ✓ **94 calories; 3.4 g fat; 13.3 g total carbohydrates; 5.8 g protein; 5.5g fiber.**

Air Fryer Chicken Milanese with Arugula

Prep Time: 15 mins; Cook Time: 15 mins;Total Time: 30 mins.
Yield: 4 Servings.

INGREDIENTS

- 2 boneless, skinless chicken breasts, (8 ounces each)
- 2 tablespoons grated Parmesan cheese
- 1 large egg, beaten
- 1 teaspoon of water
- 3/4 teaspoon kosher salt
- Freshly ground black pepper to taste
- 1/2 cup seasoned whole-wheat breadcrumbs
- olive oil spray
- 3 lemons, cut into wedges
- 1 1/2 cups baby arugula

INSTRUCTIONS

1. Cut chicken into 4 slices, then place slices between 2 sheets of parchment paper or plastic wrap and pound out to 1/4-inch thick.
2. Sprinkle both sides with salt and pepper.
3. In a shallow plate, beat the egg and 1 teaspoon of water together.
4. Combine breadcrumbs and parmesan cheese in a shallow bowl.
5. Dip the chicken into the egg, then the breadcrumb mixture. Place on a work surface and spray both sides with olive oil.
6. Preheat the air fryer to 400F.

7. In batches transfer to the air fryer basket and cook 7 minutes, turning halfway until golden and cooked through.
8. Serve chicken with 1 1/2 cups arugula and top with a generous amount of lemon juice.
9. Serve and enjoy!

NUTRITIONAL FACTS(Per Serving)

- ✓ **219 calories; 31g protein; 6g fat; 9g carbs.**

Air Fryer Basil-Parmesan Salmon

Prep Time: 5 mins Cook; Time: 15 mins;Total Time: 20 mins.

Yield: 4 Servings.

INGREDIENTS

- ❖ 4 salmon fillets, skin removed, about 5 ounces each
- ❖ 1/2 lemon
- ❖ 1/4 teaspoon Kosher salt
- ❖ freshly ground black pepper
- ❖ 3 tablespoons mayonnaise
- ❖ 6 fresh basil leaves, minced, plus more for garnish
- ❖ 3 tablespoons grated parmesan
- ❖ olive oil spray

INSTRUCTIONS

1. Preheat air fryer to 400F.
2. Spritz the basket with olive oil.
3. Season the salmon with lemon juice, salt, and pepper.
4. Mix the mayonnaise with basil and 2 tablespoons Parmesan cheese in a small bowl.
5. Spread completely over the top of salmon. Sprinkle remaining Parmesan cheese on top.
6. In batches, air fry 7 minutes, or longer depending on the thickness of the salmon.
7. Serve and enjoy!

NUTRITIONAL FACTS (Per Serving)

- ✓ **289 calories; 30g protein; 18g fat; 1g net carbs.**

Air Fryer Garlicand Parsley Baby Potatoes

Prep Time: 5 mins; Cook Time: 20 mins;Total Time: 25 mins.

Yield: 4 Servings.

INGREDIENTS

- 1 pound baby potatoes, cut into quarters
- 1 tablespoon avocado oil
- 1/4 teaspoon salt
- 1/2 teaspoon granulated garlic
- 1/2 teaspoon dried parsley

INSTRUCTIONS

1. Preheat your air fryer to 350F.
2. Combine potatoes and oil in a bowl and toss to coat.
3. Add 1/4 teaspoon granulated garlic and 1/4 teaspoon parsley and toss to coat.
4. Repeat with remaining garlic and parsley.
5. Pour potatoes into the air fryer basket.
6. Place the basket in the air fryer and cook, tossing occasionally, until golden brown, about 20 to minutes.

NUTRITION FACTS (Per Serving)

✓ 89 calories; 0.1 g fat; 14g net carbs; 2.4 g protein

AIR FRYER CRISPY BREADED PORK CHOPS

Prep Time: 10 minutes; Cook Time: 15 mins;Total Time: 25 mins.

Yield: 6 pork chops.

INGREDIENTS

- 1/2 cup panko crumbs
- 6 3/4-inch thick center-cut boneless pork chops, fat trimmed (5 ounces each)
- 1 large egg, beaten
- olive oil spray
- 1/3 cup crushed cornflakes crumbs
- 2 tablespoons grated parmesan cheese

- 1 1/4 teaspoon sweet paprika
- 1/2 teaspoon onion powder
- 1/4 teaspoon chili powder
- 1/2 teaspoon garlic powder
- 1/8 teaspoon black pepper
- 3/4 teaspoon kosher salt, more for seasoning

INSTRUCTIONS

1. Preheat the air fryer to 400F.
2. Spray the air fryer basket with oil.
3. generously season pork chops with salt on both sides.
4. Put the panko in a large bowl, add cornflake, parmesan cheese, 3/4 teaspoon salt, paprika, garlic powder, onion powder, chili powder, and black pepper. Mix well to combine.
5. Place the beaten egg in another. Dip the pork into the egg, then crumb mixture.
6. When the air fryer is ready, place 1/2 of the chops into the prepared basket and spritz the top with oil.
7. Cook for 12-15 minutes turning halfway, spritzing both sides with oil.
8. Set aside and repeat with the remaining.
9. When done, serve and enjoy!

NUTRITIONAL FACTS (Per One Pork Chop)

✓ 378 calories; 33g protein; 8g net carbs; 13g fats.

Air Fryer Zucchini Turkey Burgers

Prep Time: 10 mins; Cook Time: 10 mins;Total Time: 20 mins.

Yield: 5 burgers.

INGREDIENTS

- 1 pound 93% lean ground turkey
- 1/4 cup gluten-free breadcrumbs
- 1 clove garlic, grated
- 6 ounces grated zucchini
- 1 tablespoon grated red onion
- 1 teaspoon kosher salt
- 1 teaspoon fresh pepper

INSTRUCTIONS

1. Preheat the air fryer to 370F.
2. Use paper towels to squeeze out all the moisture from the zucchini.
3. Place the turkey and zucchini in a large bowl. Add the breadcrumbs, garlic, onion, salt, and pepper.
4. Make 5 equal patties, 4 ounces each, 1/2 inch thick.
5. Cook in the air fryer in a single layer in two batches 10 minutes, turning halfway until browned and the center is cooked through.

NUTRITIONAL FACTS (Per Burger)

✓ **161 calories; 18g protein; 4.5g carbs; 7g fat**

Air Fryer Bacon Wrapped Chicken Bites

Prep Time: 10 mins; Cook Time: 10 mins; Total Time: 20 mins.

Yield: 10 Servings.

INGREDIENTS

- 1 1/4 pounds 3 boneless skinless chicken breast, cut in 1-inch chunks
- 10 slices center-cut bacon, cut into thirds
- Serve with your favorite sauce

INSTRUCTIONS

1. Preheat the air fryer to 400F
2. Wrap a piece of bacon around each piece of chicken and secure with a toothpick.
3. Cook in batches in an even layer for 8-10 minutes, turning halfway until the chicken is cooked and the bacon is browned.
4. Blot on a paper towel and serve with your favorite sauce.

NUTRITIONAL FACTS (3 Pieces)

✓ **98 calories; 5g fats; 16g protein; 3g carbs.**

Air Fryer Cheeseburgers

Prep Time: 10 mins; Cook Time 20 mins;Total Time: 30 mins.

Yield: 4 Servings.

INGREDIENTS

- 2 cloves garlic, minced
- 1 tablespoon low-sodium soy sauce
- 1 pound ground beef
- Freshly ground black pepper to taste
- 4 slices American cheese
- Kosher salt to taste
- 4 hamburger buns
- Mayonnaise
- Lettuce
- Sliced tomatoes
- Red onion, finely sliced

INSTRUCTIONS

1. Preheat air fryer to 375F
2. In a large bowl combine beef, garlic, and soy sauce. Shape into 4 patties and flatten into a 4" circle. Season both sides with salt and pepper.
3. Place 2 patties in your air fryer and cook for 4-5 minutes per side, (4 minutes per side) for medium. Remove and immediately top with a slice of cheese.
4. Repeat with the remaining 2 patties.
5. Spread hamburger buns with mayo, then top with lettuce, patties, tomatoes, and onions.
6. Serve and enjoy!

NUTRITIONAL FACTS (Per Serving)

- **238 calories; 10g net carbs; 14g fat; 15g protein.**

Air Fryer Mozzarella Sticks

Prep Time: 5 mins; Cook Time: 8 mins;Total Time: 13 minutes.

Yield: 6 Servings.

INGREDIENTS
- 6 mozzarella sticks
- 1 cup panko bread crumbs
- Kosher salt
- Freshly cracked black pepper
- 2 large eggs, well-beaten
- 3 tablespoons all-purpose flour
- Marinara sauce

INSTRUCTIONS
1. Place mozzarella sticks in a refrigerator to freeze for about 1 hour 30 minutes.
2. Meanwhile, preheat oven to 400°F
3. Prepare three separate bowls. Place panko in one, eggs in another, and flour in the third bowl.
4. Season panko with salt and pepper.
5. Coat frozen mozzarella sticks in flour, then dip first in egg, then panko, and then again in the egg, then in the panko.
6. Arrange frozen breaded mozzarella sticks in an even layer in the basket of your air fryer. Cook for 8 minutes, or until golden and crisp on the outside and are melty in the center.
7. Serve with marinara sauce and enjoy!

NUTRITIONAL FACTS (Per Serving)
- 48 calories; 2g carbs; 2g fat; 3g protein.

Air Fryer Beef Empanadas

Prep Time: 10 mins; Cook Time: 24 mins;Total Time: 34 mins.

Yield: 6 Empanadas.

INGREDIENTS

- 8 Goya empanada discs, frozen, thawed
- 1 cup picadillo
- 1 egg white, whisked
- 1 teaspoon water

INSTRUCTIONS

1. Preheat the air fryer to 325F. Spray the basket with cooking spray.
2. Place 2 tablespoons of picadillo in the center of each disc. Fold in half and use a fork to seal the edges. Repeat with the remaining dough.
3. Whisk the egg whites with water, then brush the tops of the empanadas.
4. Working in batches, air fry 2 at a time in the air fryer for 8 minutes, or until golden.
5. Remove from heat and repeat with the remaining empanadas.
6. Serve when done and enjoy.

NUTRITIONAL FACTS (Per One Empanada)

- 183 calories; 11g protein; 5g fat; 21g net carbs.

Air Fryer Cinnamon Apple Chips

Prep Time: 5 mins; Cook Time: 24 mins;Total Time: 30 mins.

Yield: 2 Servings.

INGREDIENTS

- 2 apples, thinly sliced
- 2 teaspoons sugar
- 1/2 teaspoon cinnamon

INSTRUCTIONS

1. Preheat air fryer to 350°F
2. In a large bowl toss apples with cinnamon and sugar.
3. Working in batches, place apples in a single layer in the basket of your air fryer.

4. Bake at for about 12 minutes, flipping every 4-5 minutes.
5. When done, serve and enjoy.

NUTRITIONAL FACTS (Per Serving)
- ✓ 65 calories; 12g net carbs; 0g fat.

Crispy Avocado Fries

Prep Time: 5 mins; Cook Time: 10 mins; Total Time: 15 mins.

Yield: 4 Servings.

INGREDIENTS
- ❖ 1 cup Panko breadcrumbs
- ❖ 1 teaspoon garlic powder
- ❖ 1 teaspoon paprika
- ❖ 1 cup all-purpose flour
- ❖ 2 large eggs
- ❖ 2 avocados, sliced
- ❖ Ranch, for serving (optional)

INSTRUCTIONS
1. Preheat air fryer to 400°F
2. In a shallow bowl, whisk together Panko, garlic powder, and paprika. Place flour in another shallow bowl, and in a third shallow bowl beat eggs.
3. One at a time, dip avocado slices into flour, then egg, then Panko mixture until fully coated.
4. Place in the air fryer and fry for 10 minutes.
5. Serve with ranch, if desired.

NUTRITIONAL FACTS (Per Serving)
- ✓ 191 calories; 6g fat; 26g net carbs; 4g protein.

Air Fried Shishito Peppers

Prep Time: 2 mins; Cook Time: 8 mins;Total Time: 10 mins.

Yield;d: 4 Servings.

INGREDIENTS
- 8 ounces shishito peppers
- extra virgin olive oil spray
- 1/4 teaspoon kosher salt
- 1 lemon, cut into wedges

INSTRUCTIONS
1. Preheat the air fryer 400F.
2. Spritz the shishito peppers all over with olive oil.
3. Transfer the shishito peppers to the air fryer and cook 8 minutes, shaking the basket halfway until soft and slightly charred and blistered
4. Sprinkle with salt and squeeze with lemon wedges, serve and enjoy.

NUTRITIONAL FACTS(Per Serving)
- 15 calories; 2g protein; 2g net carbs.

Air Fryer Salmon with Maple Soy Glaze and Garlic

Prep Time: 5 mins; Cook Time: 10 mins; Marinate Time: 20 mins;Total Time: 35 mins.

Yield: 4 Servings.

INGREDIENTS
- 4 skinless salmon fillets (24 ounces)
- 3 tablespoons pure maple syrup
- 3 tablespoons reduced gluten-free soy sauce
- 1 clove garlic, smashed
- 1 tablespoon sriracha hot sauce

INSTRUCTIONS
1. Put the maple syrup into a small bowl add soy sauce and mix. Add sriracha and garlic, mix well to combine and then pour the mixture into a gallon-sized resealable bag and add the salmon.

2. Marinate 20 minutes, turning once in a while.
3. Preheat air fryer to 400F. Lightly spray the basket with nonstick spray.
4. Remove the fish from the marinade, reserving and pat dry with paper towels.
5. Place the fish in the air fryer, in batches, air fry for 8 minutes.
6. Meanwhile, pour the marinade in a small saucepan and bring to a simmer over medium-low heat and reduce until it thickens into a glaze, 2 minutes.
7. Spoon over salmon, serve and enjoy.

NUTRITIONAL FACTS (Per Serving)
- ✓ 292 calories; 35g protein; 11g fat; 11.5g net carbs.

Parmesan Fried Tortellini

Prep Time: 5 mins; Cook Time: 20 mins; Total Time: 25 mins.

Yield: 6 Servings.

INGREDIENTS
- ❖ 1 package cheese tortellini (about 9 ounces)
- ❖ 1 cup Panko breadcrumbs
- ❖ 1/3 cup freshly grated Parmesan
- ❖ 1 teaspoon dried oregano
- ❖ 1/2 teaspoon garlic powder
- ❖ 1/2 teaspoon crushed red pepper flakes
- ❖ Kosher salt
- ❖ Freshly ground black pepper
- ❖ 1 cup all-purpose flour
- ❖ 2 large eggs
- ❖ Marinara, for serving

INSTRUCTIONS
1. In a large pot of boiling salted water, cook tortellini according to package instructions until al dente. Drain.
2. In a shallow bowl, mix together Panko, Parmesan, oregano, garlic powder, and red pepper flakes. Season with salt and pepper. In another shallow bowl, beat eggs, and in a third shallow bowl, add flour.
3. Coat tortellini in flour, then dredge in eggs, then in Panko mixture. Continue until all tortellini are coated.
4. Place in an air fryer and fry at 370° until crispy, 10 minutes.

5. Serve with marinara.

NUTRITIONAL FACTS (Per Serving)

- ✓ 440 calories; 26g fat; 25g carbs; 13g protein.

Garlic Parmesan Chicken

Prep Time: 5 mins; Cook Time: 25 mins; Total Time: 30 mins.

Yields: 4 servings.

INGREDIENTS

- ❖ 4 bone-in chicken thighs, skin-on (about 2 pounds)
- ❖ Kosher salt
- ❖ Freshly ground black pepper
- ❖ 1 cup Panko breadcrumbs
- ❖ 1 teaspoon garlic powder
- ❖ 1 teaspoon Italian seasoning
- ❖ 2/3 cup freshly grated Parmesan
- ❖ 2 large eggs

INSTRUCTIONS

1. Season chicken with salt and pepper. In a shallow bowl, whisk together panko, garlic powder, Italian seasoning, and Parmesan. In another shallow bowl, beat eggs.
2. Dip chicken thighs in egg, then roll in the panko mixture until fully coated.
3. Cook in the air fryer at 360° for about 25 minutes or until golden and cooked through.
4. When done, take out of the fryer and serve.

NUTRITIONAL FACTS (Per Serving)

- ✓ 440 calories; 26g fat; 25g carbs; 13g protein.

Air Fried Sweet Potato Hash

Prep Time: 10 mins; Cook Time: 15 mins;Total Time: 25 mins.

Yield: 6 Servings.

INGREDIENTS
- 2 large sweet potato, cut into small cubes
- 2 slices bacon, cut into small pieces
- 1 tablespoon smoked paprika
- 2 tablespoons olive oil
- 1 teaspoon dried dill weed
- 1 teaspoon sea salt
- 1 teaspoon ground black pepper

INSTRUCTIONS
1. Preheat an air fryer to 400 F.
2. In a large bowl combine sweet potato, bacon and olive oil and mix. Add paprika, dill, salt, and pepper. Mix well until the mixture is well combined.
3. Place mixture into the preheated air fryer.
4. Cook for about 15 minutes or until crispy and browned.
5. Serve warm and enjoy.

NUTRITIONAL FACTS (Per Serving)
- 191 calories; 6g fat; 26g net carbs; 4g protein.

Air Fryer Cinnamon and Sugar Doughnuts

Prep Time: 25 mins; Cook Time: 15 mins;Total 40 mins.

Yield: 9 Doughnuts.

INGREDIENTS
- 2 1/4 cups all-purpose flour
- 2 1/2 tablespoons butter, at room temperature
- 1 1/2 teaspoons baking powder
- 2 large egg yolks
- 1/2 cup white sugar
- 1 teaspoon salt
- 1/2 cup sour cream

- 1/3 cup white sugar
- 1 teaspoon cinnamon
- 2 tablespoons butter, melted

INSTRUCTIONS

1. into the basket of the air fryer; cook for 8 minutes. Place 1/2 cup whitesugar into a bowl. Add 2 1/2 tablespoons butter and mix until crumbly. Add egg yolksand stir tocombine.
2. In a different bowl add flour, baking powder, and salt. Add 1/3 of the flour mixture and 1/2 thesour cream into the sugar-egg mixture; stir until well combined. Mix in the remaining flour and sour cream. Refrigerate dough until ready to use.
3. Mix 1/3 cupsugar and cinnamon together in a bowl.
4. Roll dough out onto a lightly floured work surface to 1/2-inch thick. Cut 9 large circles in the dough; cut a small circleout of the center of each large circle tocreate doughnut shapes.
5. Preheat air fryer to 350 F.
6. Brush 1/2 of the melted butter over both sidesof the doughnuts.
7. Place 1/2 doughnuts
8. Grease cooked donuts with the remaining melted butter and dip into thecinnamon-sugar mixture.
9. Repeat with the remaining doughnuts.Serve!

NUTRITIONAL FACTS (Per Doughnuts)

- **276 calories; 43g carbs; 1g fiber; 5g protein; 10g fats.**

Air Fryer Garlicand Parsley Baby Potatoes

Prep Time: 5 mins; Cook Time: 20 mins;Total Time: 25 mins.

Yield: 4 Servings.

INGREDIENTS

- 1 pound baby potatoes, cut into quarters
- 1 tablespoon avocado oil
- 1/4 teaspoon salt
- 1/2 teaspoon granulated garlic
- 1/2 teaspoon dried parsley

INSTRUCTIONS

1. Preheat an air fryer to 350 F.
2. Combine potatoes and oil in a bowl and toss to coat. Add 1/4 teaspoon granulated garlic and 1/4 teaspoon parsley and toss to coat. Repeat with remaining garlic and parsley. Pour potatoes into the air fryer basket.
3. Place the basket in the air fryer and cook for about 20 mins, tossing occasionally, until golden brown.

NUTRITIONAL FACTS (Per Serving)

✓ **89 calories; 4g protein; 1g fat; 20g carbs; 3g fiber.**

Air Fried Hot Dogs

Prep Time: 3 mins; Cook Time: 7 mins; Total Time: 10 mins.

Yield: 2 Servings.

INGREDIENTS

- 2 hot dog buns
- 2 hot dogs
- 2 tablespoons grated cheese

INSTRUCTIONS

1. Preheat air fryer to 390 F for about 4 minutes.
2. Place two hot dogs into the air fryer and cook for about 5 minutes.
3. Remove the hot dog from the air fryer.
4. Place the hot dog on a bun, add cheese and put back into the air fryer, and then cook for another 2 minutes.
5. Serve and enjoy.

NUTRITIONAL FACTS (Per Serving)

✓ **289 calories; 12g protein; 13g fat; 29g carbs.**

Air Fried Avocado Egg Rolls

Prep Time: 15 mins; Cook Time: 15 mins; Total Time: 30 mins.

Yield: 10 Avocado Eggrolls.

INGREDIENTS

- Egg Rolls
- 12 ounces from 3 medium avocados, cubed
- 10 egg roll wrappers
- Juice from 2 small limes
- ¼ cup chopped sundried tomatoes, packed in oil, drained
- 2/3 cup diced red onion
- 1/3 cup chopped cilantro
- 1 teaspoon kosher salt
- Freshly ground black pepper to taste
- A small bowl of water for sealing
- Olive oil spray

Dipping Sauce

- 2 tablespoons mayonnaise
- 1 tablespoon sweet chili sauce
- 2-3 teaspoons sriracha sauce

INSTRUCTIONS

1. Preheat the air fryer to 400F. In a medium bowl, combine avocado, lime juice, onion, tomatoes, cilantro, salt and pepper. Mix until well combined.
2. One at a time, place egg roll wrapper on a clean surface, points facing top and bottom like a diamond. Spoon ¼ cup mixture onto the bottom third of the wrapper.
3. Dip your finger in a small bowl of water and run it along the edges of the wrapper.
4. Lift the point nearest you and wrap it around the filling. Fold the left and right corners in toward the center and continue to roll into a tight cylinder. Set aside and repeat with remaining wrappers and filling. Spray all sides of the egg rolls with oil.
5. In batches, cook for 6 minutes, turning halfway through, or until golden.
6. Meanwhile, in another bowl, combine mayonnaise, sweet chili sauce, and sriracha and serve on the side for dipping.

NUTRITIONAL FACTS (Per Eggroll)

- 148 calories; 14g net carbs; 1g fat; 4g protein.

Air Fried Crumbed Chicken Tenderloins

Prep Time: 15 mins; Cook Time: 15 mins; Total Time: 30 mins.

Yield: 8 Servings.

INGREDIENTS

- 8 chicken tenderloins
- 1 egg
- ½ cup dry bread crumbs
- 2 tablespoons olive oil

INSTRUCTIONS

1. Preheat air fryer to 350 F.
2. Whisk egg in a small bowl.
3. Mix bread crumbs and oil together in another bowl until the mixture becomes loose and crumbly.
4. Dip each of the tenderloins in the egg mixture; then dip into the crumb mixture, making sure each tenderloin is well coated.
5. Arrange chicken tenderloins in the air fryer basket.
6. Cook for 12-15 minutes or until no longer pink in the center.
7. Serve and enjoy.

NUTRITIONAL FACTS (Per Tenderloin)

- **243 calories; 26g protein; 11.4g fats; 9.8g carbs.**

Air Fried Ribeye Steak

Prep Time: 25 mins; Cook Time: 10 mins; Total Time: 35 mins.

Yield: 2 servings.

INGREDIENTS

- 1/2 teaspoon ground coffee
- 1 pound ribeye steak
- 1 teaspoon brown sugar
- 1/2 teaspoon black pepper
- 1/4 teaspoon paprika
- 1/4 teaspoon chili powder
- 1/4 teaspoon garlic powder

- ❖ 1/4 teaspoon onion powder
- ❖ 1/4 teaspoon chipotle powder
- ❖ 1/8 teaspoon coriander
- ❖ 1 1/2 teaspoons coarse sea salt
- ❖ 1/8 teaspoon cocoa powder

INSTRUCTIONS

1. Place all the spices in a small bowl and mix well to combine, making sure the brown sugar is well crushed.
2. Sprinkle a generous amount of spice mix onto a plate. Lay one steak on top of spices. Then season steak liberally with spice mix and rub into the meat evenly. Flip to make sure the other side is seasoned properly as well.
3. Let steak sit for about 20 minutes.
4. Prepare air fryer tray by coating with the oil to prevent sticking. Preheat air fryer to 390 F for at least 3 minutes.
5. Cook steak for 9 minutes.
6. When done cooking, remove from the air fryer and allow it to cool for at least 5 minutes before slicing.
7. Slice, serve with your favorite sauce and enjoy.

NUTRITIONAL FACTS (Per Serving)

- ✓ **495 calories; 32g fat; 5g carbs; 46g protein**

Fried Asparagus with Spicy Mayo Dip

Prep Time: 20 mins; Cook Time: 5 mins;Total Time; 25 mins.

Yield: 2 Servings.

INGREDIENTS

- ❖ 10 fresh asparagus spears
- ❖ olive oil for frying

Egg Wash

- ❖ 1 large egg
- ❖ 1 tablespoon heavy whipping cream

Breading

- ❖ 1/3 cup blanched almond flour
- ❖ 1/3 cup finely grated parmesan cheese

- ❖ 1/2 teaspoon paprika
- ❖ 1/2 teaspoon salt

Dipping Sauce

- ❖ 1 teaspoon Dijon mustard
- ❖ 1/4 cup mayonnaise
- ❖ 1/4 teaspoon cayenne
- ❖ 1/4 teaspoon black pepper

INSTRUCTIONS

1. In a small bowl, combine the Dijon, mayo, cayenne, and black pepper together. Mix until well combined. Refrigerate until ready to use.
2. Cut off the tough woody ends of the asparagus spears so you're left with about 6 inches. Rinse and dry them.
3. Beat the egg and heavy cream together in a bowl until well-mixed.
4. Pour the mixture into a shallow plate.
5. Combine the almond flour, cheese, paprika, and salt together in a shallow plate or bowl. Stir together until well-mixed.
6. Generously coat each asparagus spear in the egg wash with your first hand, then in the breading with your second hand until well-coated on all sides. Gently shake off excess and transfer to wax or parchment paper. Repeat with the other asparagus spears.
7. Meanwhile, preheat air fryer for some minutes. Add oil to heat up.
8. Working in batches, air fry the breaded asparagus until golden brown, 3 to 5 minutes, and drain on paper towels. You may need to work in batches to avoid overcrowding.
9. Serve with the dip and enjoy it.

NUTRITIONAL FACTS (Per Serving)

✓ **420 calories; 3.5g net carbs; 9g protein; 40g fat.**

Air Fryer Zucchini Chips

Prep Time: 10 mins; Cook Time: 25 mins; Total Time: 35 mins.

Yield: 4 Servings.

INGREDIENTS
- 1 cup panko bread crumbs
- 3/4 cup grated Parmesan cheese
- 1 medium zucchini, thinly sliced
- 1 large egg, beaten
- cooking spray

INSTRUCTIONS
1. Preheat air fryer to 350 F.
2. Combine panko and Parmesan cheese on a plate. Dip 1 zucchini slice into beaten egg then into the panko mixture, pressing to coat.
3. Place zucchini slice on a wire baking rack and repeat with remaining slices. Spray zucchini slices with cooking spray.
4. Place zucchini slices in the air fryer basket. Do not overcrowd.
5. Cook for 10 minutes, flip with tongs and cook for 2 minutes more.
6. Remove from air fryer and repeat with remaining zucchini slices.
7. Serve.

NUTRITIONAL FACTS (Per Serving)
- 159 calories; 10.8g protein; 6.6g fat; 20g carbs.

Air Fried Coconut Shrimp

Prep Time: 10 mins; Cook Time: 15 mins; Total Time: 25 mins.

Yield: 4 Servings.

INGREDIENTS
- 1/4 cup cornstarch
- 1 teaspoon salt
- 2 egg whites
- 1 cup flaked sweetened coconut
- 1/2 pound large raw shrimp

INSTRUCTIONS

1. Preheat air fryer to 330 F.
2. In a shallow bowl, combine the cornstarch and salt.
3. In a second shallow bowl, add the egg whites
4. In a third shallow bowl, add the coconut
5. Working with one shrimp at a time, dredge in the cornstarch mixture, then egg whites, then coconut.
6. Spray air fryer with non-stick cooking spray. Add shrimp to the air fryer basket. Air fry for 10-15 minutes.
7. Repeat until all shrimp are cooked.

NUTRITIONAL FACTS (Per Serving)

✓ **191 calories; 16g carbs; 6g fat; 13g protein**

Air Fried Corn on the Cob

Prep Time: 10 mins; Cook Time: 10 mins;Total Time: 20 mins.
Yield: 4 pieces of corn.

INGREDIENTS

- 2 ears corn, shucked and halved
- 2 teaspoons crumbled cotija cheese
- 1/4 cup mayonnaise
- 1 teaspoon lime juice
- 1/4 teaspoon chili powder
- 4 sprigs fresh cilantro, optional

INSTRUCTIONS

1. Preheat your air fryer to 400 F.
2. Mix the mayo, cheese, lime, and chili powder in a bowl.
3. Roll each piece of corn in the mayonnaise mixture until all sides are completely coated.
4. Place all 4 pieces of the corn in the air fryer basket and cook for 8 minutes.
5. Garnish with cilantro.
6. Enjoy!

NUTRITIONAL FACTS (Per Piece Of Corn)

✓ **144 calories; 8g net carbs; 2g protein; 12g fat**

Air-Fried Butter Cake

Prep Time: 10 mins; Cook Time: 15 mins;Total Time: 25 mins.
Yield: 4 Servings.

INGREDIENTS

- 7 tablespoons butter, at room temperature
- 1 2/3 cups all-purpose flour
- 1/4 cup white sugar
- 1 egg
- 2 tablespoons white sugar
- 1 pinch salt, or to taste
- 6 tablespoons milk
- Cooking spray

INSTRUCTIONS

1. Preheat an air fryer to 356F.
2. Spray a small fluted tube pan with cooking spray.
3. Place butter and all the sugar ina bowl and mix together using an electric mixer until light and creamy. Add egg and mix until smooth and fluffy.
4. Stir in flour and salt. Add milk and mix thoroughly. Transfer the mixture to the prepared pan; use the back of a spoon to level the surface.
5. Place the pan in the air fryer basket and air fry 15 mins.
6. Turn cake out of the pan and allow it to cool for about 5 minutes.
7. Enjoy!

NUTRITIONAL FACTS (Per Serving)

- 470 calories; 22.4g fat; 8g protein; 58g carbs.

Air Fryer Beef Satay

Prep&Marinate Time: 10& 30 mins; Cook Time: 40 mins;Total Time: 1 hour 20 mins.
Yield: 2 servings.

INGREDIENTS

- 1 pound beef flank steak sliced thinly into long strips
- 1 tablespoon Fish Sauce
- 1 tablespoon minced ginger
- 1 tablespoon Minced Garlic

- 2 tablespoons oil
- 1 tablespoon Soy Sauce
- 1 teaspoon Sriracha Sauce
- 1 teaspoon Ground Coriander
- 1 tablespoon sugar
- 1/4 cup chopped roasted peanuts
- 1/2 cup chopped cilantro divided

INSTRUCTIONS

1. Place beef strips into a ziplock bag.
2. Add oil, fish sauce, soy sauce, ginger, garlic, sugar, Sriracha, coriander, and 1/4 cup cilantro and mix well. Marinate for 30 minutes.
3. Preheat your air fryer to 200 C.
4. Using a set of tongs, place the beef strips in the air fryer basket in a single layer.
5. Leave behind as much of the marinade as you can and discard this marinade.
6. Place in the air fryer basket and air fry for 8-10 mins, flipping once halfway.
7. Remove the meat to a serving tray, top with remaining 1/4 cup chopped cilantro and the chopped roasted peanuts.
8. Serve with your choice of sauce

NUTRITIONAL FACTS (Per Serving)

- ✓ 159 calories; 26g fat; 11g carbs; 13g protein

Keto Air Fried Chicken Meatballs

Prep Time: 10 mins; Cook Time: 15 mins;Total Time: 25 mins.
Yield: 4 Servings.

INGREDIENTS

- 1 pound Ground Chicken
- 1/2 cup cilantro, chopped
- 2 Green Onions finely chopped
- 1 tablespoon Soy Sauce
- 1 teaspoon Sriracha Sauce
- 1 teaspoon Sesame Oil
- 1/4 cup Unsweetened Shredded Coconut
- Salt to taste
- 1 tablespoon Hoisin Sauce
- Ground Black Pepper to taste

INSTRUCTIONS

1. Gently mix all ingredients together in a bowl.
2. Prepare an air fryer tray by coating with the oil to prevent sticking.
3. Preheat air fryer to 176 C for at least 3 minutes.
4. Working in batches, scoop some rounds of the mixture into the air fryer.
5. Cook by air frying for 10 minutes, flipping once until they reach an internal temperature of 150-165F.
6. If desired, increase heat to 200 C and cook for 2 more minutes or until tops are browned.

NUTRITIONAL FACTS (Per Serving)

✓ 223 calories; 20g protein; 2g net carbs; 14g fat.

Air-Fryer Roasted Veggies

Prep Time: 20 mins; Cook Time: 10 mins; Total Time: 30 mins.
Yield: 4 Servings.

INGREDIENTS

- ❖ 1/2 cup diced asparagus
- ❖ 1/2 cup diced mushrooms
- ❖ 1/2 cup diced zucchini
- ❖ 1/2 cup diced summer squash
- ❖ 2 teaspoons vegetable oil
- ❖ 1/2 cup diced cauliflower
- ❖ 1/4 teaspoon salt
- ❖ 1/2 cup diced sweet red pepper
- ❖ 1/4 teaspoon ground black pepper
- ❖ 1/4 teaspoon Italian seasoning

INSTRUCTIONS

1. Preheat your air fryer to 356 F.
2. Add all the ingredients in a bowl and mix until well combined
3. Arrange in the fryer basket.
4. Cook for 10 minutes, stirring after every 3-4 minutes.

NUTRITIONAL FACTS (Per Serving)

✓ 37 calories; 2g net carbs; 1.3g fiber; 2.4g fat; 1.5g protein.

Air Fryer Steak with Garlic Herb Butter

Prep Tim: 20 mins; Cook Time: 15 mins;Total Time: 35 mins.

Yield: 2 Servings.

INGREDIENTS

- 2 (8 ounces Ribeye steak
- Vegetable oil
- Salt to taste
- Freshly cracked black pepper

Garlic Butter

- 1 stick unsalted butter softened
- 2 tablespoons fresh parsley chopped
- 2 teaspoons garlic minced
- 1 teaspoon Worcestershire Sauce
- 1/2 teaspoon salt

INSTRUCTIONS

1. Prepare Garlic Butter by mixing butter, parsley garlic, Worcestershire sauce, and salt until thoroughly combined.
2. Place in parchment paper and roll into a log. Refrigerate until ready to use.
3. Remove steak from the fridge and allow to sit at room temperature for 20 minutes. Rub a little bit of olive oil on both sides of the steak and season with salt and freshly cracked black pepper.
4. Grease your Air Fryer with oil.
5. Preheat Air Fryer to 400 F and cook for 15 minutes or until cooked through to your liking, flipping halfway through.
6. Remove from the air fryer and allow it to rest for 5 minutes.
7. Top with garlic butter.
8. Serve and enjoy

NUTRITIONAL FACTS (Per Serving)

- ✓ **220 calories; 20g protein; 2g net carbs; 14g fat.**

Air Fryer Eggplant Parmesan

Prep Time: 15 mins; Cook Time: 25 mins;Total Time: 40 mins.

Yield: 4 Servings.

INGREDIENTS

- 1 large eggplant mine (about 1 1/4 pounds)
- 1/2 cup whole wheat bread crumbs
- 3 tablespoons finely grated parmesan cheese
- Salt to taste
- 1 teaspoon Italian seasoning mix
- 3 tablespoons whole wheat flour
- 1 egg + 1 tbsp water
- olive oil spray
- 1 cup marinara sauce
- 1/4 cup grated mozzarella cheese
- fresh parsley or basil to garnish

INSTRUCTIONS

1. Cut eggplant into ½ inch slices. Rub some salt on both sides of the slices and leave it for at least 10-15 mins.
2. Meanwhile in a small bowl mix egg with water and flour to prepare the batter.
3. In a medium shallow plate combine bread crumbs, parmesan cheese, Italian seasoning blend, and some salt. Mix thoroughly.
4. Now apply the batter to each eggplant slice evenly.
5. Dip the battered slices in the breadcrumb mix to coat it evenly on all sides.
6. Place breaded eggplant slices on a clean and dry flat plate and spray oil on them.
7. Preheat the Air Fryer to 360 F. Then put the eggplant slices on the wire mesh and cook for about 8 min.
8. Top the air fried slices with about 1 tablespoon of marinara sauce and lightly spread fresh mozzarella cheese on it. Cook the eggplant for another 1-2 min or until the cheese melts.
9. Serve warm on the side of your favorite pasta.

NUTRITIONAL FACTS (Per Serving)

- 193 calories; 5.5g fat; 20g carbs; 10g protein.

Low Carb Air Fried Onion Rings

Prep Time: 10 mins; Cook Time: 16 mins; Total Time: 26 mins.

Yield: 4 Servings.

INGREDIENTS
- 1 onion sliced
- 1 1/4 cup flour
- 1 tablespoon baking powder
- 1 egg, beaten
- 3/4 cup bread crumbs
- 1 cup + 1 teaspoon milk
- Seasonings of choice

INSTRUCTIONS
1. Preheat air fryer to 370 F.
2. Place the flour, baking powder and seasonings in a mixing bowl and mix together. Add the egg and mix add the milk. Mix all together until well combined.
3. Transfer the mixture to a shallow bowl.
4. Place the bread crumbs in another shallow bowl.
5. Following the dredging pattern, use a fork to pick one slice of onion and cover it fully with the content of the first bowl, and then the second bowl. Following a similar procedure, repeat for other onion slices.
6. Arrange the onions rings in the air fryer and air fry for 8 minutes, flip over and then fry for another 8 minutes.

NUTRITIONAL FACTS (Per Serving)
- 172 calories; 4g fat; 14g net carbs; 11g protein.

Air Fryer French Toast Sticks

Prep Time: 10 mins; Cook Time: 10 mins; Total Time: 20 mins.

Yield: 2 Servings.

INGREDIENTS
- 4 slices slightly stale thick bread, such as Texas toast
- parchment paper
- 2 eggs, lightly beaten

- ❖ 1/4 cup milk
- ❖ 1 teaspoon vanilla extract
- ❖ 1 teaspoon cinnamon
- ❖ 1 pinch ground nutmeg (optional)

INSTRUCTIONS

1. Cut each slice of bread into thirds to make sticks. Cut a piece of parchment paper to fit the bottom of the air fryer basket.
2. Preheat air fryer to 180 C.
3. Stir together eggs, milk, vanilla, cinnamon, and nutmeg in a bowl until well combined. Dip each piece of bread into the egg mixture, making sure each piece is well submerged. Shake each breadstick to remove excess liquid and place in a single layer in the air fryer basket.
4. Cooking in batches, Cook for 5 minutes, turn bread pieces, and cook for an additional 5 minutes.

NUTRITIONAL FACTS (Per Serving)

✓ **231 calories; 28.6g carbs; 1.9g fiber; 11.2g protein; 8g fat.Air.**

Fryer Sausage Patties

Prep Time: 5 mins Cook Time: 10 mins:Total Time: 15 mins.

Yield: 4 Servings.

INGREDIENTS

- ❖ 1 (12 ounces) package sausage patties
- ❖ Nonstick cooking spray

INSTRUCTIONS

1. Preheat air fryer to 400 F.
2. Place sausage patties into the basket in a single layer.
3. Cook in the air fryer for 5 minutes.
4. Flip the sausage over and cook for another 3-4 minutes or until an instant-read thermometer inserted into the center of a patty reads 70 C.

NUTRITIONAL FACTS(Per Serving)

✓ **145 calories; 9g fat; 0.7g net carbs; 14g protein.**

Air Fried Buffalo Cauliflower Bites

Prep Time: 5 mins; Cook Time: 10 mins; Total Time: 15 mins.

Yield: 4 Servings.

INGREDIENTS
- 1 egg
- 1 cup panko crumbs
- 1/2 head cauliflower
- 1/2 teaspoon salt
- 1/2 teaspoon garlic powder
- freshly ground black pepper
- 1 cup ranch dressing
- 1/2 cup hot sauce

INSTRUCTIONS
1. Separate cauliflower to florets. Dip them in the egg, mixed with salt, garlic powder, and pepper. Then dip into panko breadcrumbs.
2. Preheat air fryer to 400 degrees. Add all the cauliflower to the basket and cook for 8-10 minutes. Shake halfway through.
3. Meanwhile mix ranch with hot sauce. Serve on the side.

NUTRITIONAL FACTS (Per Serving)
- 94 calories; 12g net carbs; 4g protein; 2g fat.

Air Fryer Fish and Chips

Prep Time: 10 mins Cook; Time: 35 mins; Total Time: 45 mins.

Yield: 4 Servings.

INGREDIENTS
- 1 pound catfish fillet (or your choice fish)
- 1 cup breadcrumbs
- 1 egg
- 1/4 cup flour
- 1 teaspoon salt
- 2 teaspoons oil
- 2 russet potatoes

INSTRUCTIONS

1. Cut potatoes in wedges or like French fries.
2. In a bowl, toss together potatoes. salt and oil.
3. Add potatoes into your air fryer basket and cook
4. on 2000C for 20 minutes, shaking twice.
5. Once done remove from the basket.
6. Meanwhile, prepare the fish. In a shallow bowl add flour, in a second bowl add beaten egg and in the third bowl add breadcrumbs.
7. Working with one piece at a time, dredge fish fillet first in flour, then in egg, and then in breadcrumbs.
8. Add fish to the air fryer and set it to 330F for 15 minutes.
9. Check on it halfway through and flip if needed.
10. Serve together with any sauce of your choice.

NUTRITIONAL FACTS (Per Serving)

✓ 409 calories; 44g total carbs; 1g fiber; 11g fat; 30g protein.

Air Fried Okra

Prep Time: 15 mins; Cook Time: 15 mins; Total Time: 30 mins.

Yield: 4 servings.

INGREDIENTS

- 7 ounces fresh okra
- 1 egg
- 1 cup skim milk
- 1 cup breadcrumbs
- 1/2 teaspoon sea salt
- Oil for cooking spray

INSTRUCTIONS

1. Remove stem ends from okra and cut in 1/2 inch slices.
2. In a medium bowl, beat together egg and milk. Add okra slices and stir to coat.
3. In a sealable plastic bag or container with lid, mix together the breadcrumbs and salt.
4. Remove okra from egg mixture, letting excess drip off, and transfer into the bag with breadcrumbs. Be sure okra is well-drained before placing it in the breadcrumbs.

5. Use a slotted spoon to lift a little okra at a time and let plenty of the egg wash drip off before putting it into the breadcrumb mixture.
6. Shake okra in crumbs to coat well.
7. Place all of the coated okra in your air fryer basket and spritz.
8. Cook on 400F for 5 minutes. Shake basket to redistribute and give it another oil spritz as you shake.
9. Cook 5 more minutes. Shake and spray again. Cook for 3 to 5 minutes longer or until golden brown and crispy.

NUTRITIONAL FACTS (Per Serving)
- ✓ 151 calories; 7g protein; 5g net carbs; 12g fat.

Air Fryer Chicken Wings

Prep Time: 10 mins; Cook Time: 15 mins; Total Time: 25 mins.

Yield: 4 Servings.

INGREDIENTS
- ❖ 2 pounds chicken wings cut into drumettes and flats
- ❖ ½ cup grated Parmesan Cheese, plus more for garnish
- ❖ 1 teaspoon paprika
- ❖ 1 teaspoon Herbes de Provence
- ❖ Salt
- ❖ Cooking spray

INSTRUCTIONS
1. Pat chicken wings dry and set aside in a bowl.
2. In a small bowl mix the Parmesan, Paprika, Herbes de Provence and salt.
3. Coat the wings in your Parmesan mix.
4. Preheat air fryer to 350F and then spray the basket with cooking spray.
5. Cook the chicken wings in batches for 15 mins, turning halfway through.
6. Using a meat thermometer, test the temperature of the chicken wing to make sure it has reached 165 F.
7. Garnish with extra Parmesan and fresh herbs.
8. Serve and enjoy.

NUTRITIONAL FACTS (Per Serving)
- ✓ 328 calories; 23g fat; 27g protein.

Air Fryer Sweet Potato Tots

Prep Time: 15 mins; Cook Time: 35 mins; Total Time: 1 hour.

Yield: 24 Servings.

INGREDIENTS

- 2 sweet potatoes, peeled
- 1/2 teaspoon Cajun seasoning
- olive oil cooking spray
- Sea salt to taste

INSTRUCTIONS

1. Bring a pot of water to a boil and add potatoes. Boil about 15 minutes or until potatoes can be pierced with a fork but are still firm. Be careful not to over-boil. Drain and let cool.
2. Grate sweet potatoes into a bowl using a box grater. Carefully mix in Cajun seasoning. Form mixture into tot-shaped cylinders.
3. Spray the air fryer basket with olive oil spray. Place tots in the basket in a single row without touching each other or the sides of the basket. Spray tots with olive oil spray and sprinkle with sea salt.
4. Heat air fryer to 400 degrees F and cook tots for 8 minutes.
5. Flip tots over, spray with more olive oil and sprinkle with more sea salt. Cook for another 8 minutes more.

NUTRITIONAL FACTS (Per Serving)

- ✓ **21 calories; 4g net carbs; 0.4g protein.**

Air Fryer Coconut Pie Recipe (Gluten-Free)

Prep Time: 7 mins; Cook Time: 12 mins; Total Time: 19 mins.

Yield: 7 Servings.

INGREDIENTS

- 2 eggs
- 1 1/2 cups almond milk
- 1/4 cup butter
- 1 1/2 teaspoons vanilla extract

- 1 cup shredded coconut
- 1/2 cup granulated Monk Fruit
- 1/2 cup coconut flour

INSTRUCTIONS

1. Coat a 6-inch pie plate with nonstick spray and set aside.
2. Place all the ingredients in a large bowl and stir well to blend.
3. Preheat air fryer to 350 F.
4. Pour the batter into the prepared pie plate and cook in the air fryer for 12 minutes.
5. Check the pie halfway through the cooking time to be sure it is not burning, give the plate a turn, flip over and continue cooking.

NUTRITIONAL FACTS (Per Serving)

- 21 calories; 4g net carbs; 4g protein; 6g fat

Air Fried Bacon and Cream Cheese Stuffed Jalapeno Poppers

Prep Time: 10 mins; Cook Time: 5 mins; Total Time: 15 mins.

Yield: 5 Servings.

INGREDIENTS

- 10 fresh jalapenos
- 6 ounces cream cheese
- 1/4 cup shredded cheddar cheese
- 2 slices cooked bacon, crumbled
- Cooking oil spray

INSTRUCTIONS

1. Slice the jalapenos in half, vertically, to create 2 halves per jalapeno.
2. Place the cream cheese in a bowl. Microwave for 15 seconds to soften.
3. Remove the seeds and the inside of the jalapeno. (You may want to reserve some of the seeds if you prefer spicy poppers)
4. Combine the cream cheese, crumbled bacon, and shredded cheese in a bowl. Mix well.
5. For extra spicy poppers, add the reserved seeds to the cream cheese mixture, and mix well.

6. Stuff each of the jalapenos with the cream cheese mixture.
7. Preheat air fryer to 370 F.
8. Place the poppers into the Air Fryer and spray with cooking oil.
9. Cook the poppers for 5 minutes.
10. Remove from the Air Fryer and cool before serving.
11. Enjoy!

NUTRITIONAL FACTS (Per Serving)

✓ 62 calories; 4g fat; 3g net carbs; 3g protein

Cilantro Ranch Sweet Potato Cauliflower Patties

Prep Time: 15 mins; Cook Time: 20 mins; Total Time: 35 mins.

Yield: 7 Patties.

INGREDIENTS
- 1 large sweet potato, peeled
- 2 cup cauliflower florets
- 1 green onion, chopped.
- 1 teaspoon minced garlic
- 2 tablespoons organic ranch seasoning mix
- 1 cup packed fresh cilantro
- 1/2 teaspoon chili powder
- 1/4 teaspoon cumin
- 2 tablespoons gluten-free flour of choice
- 1/4 cup ground flaxseed
- 1/4 cup pumpkin seeds
- 1/4 teaspoon Kosher Salt
- pepper to taste
- Dipping sauce of choice

INSTRUCTIONS

1. Cut the peeled sweet potato into smaller pieces. Place in a food processor or blender and pulse until the larger pieces are broken up.
2. Add in your cauliflower, onion, and garlic and pulse again.
3. Add the sunflower seeds, flaxseed, flour, cilantro, and remaining seasonings. Pulse or place on medium until a thick batter is formed.

4. Place batter in a larger bowl. Scoop 1/4 cup of the batter out at a time and form into patties about 1.5 inches thick. Place on a baking sheet.
5. Repeat until you have about 7-10 patties.
6. Chill in a freezer for 10 minutes so the patties can set, flipping halfway.
7. Preheat your air fryer to 360 F.
8. Working in batches, place 4 cauliflower patties in the air fryer and cook for 18 minutes, flipping halfway.

NUTRITIONAL FACTS (Per Patty)
- ✓ 85 calories; 5.5g net carbs; 3g fat;3g protein.

Keto Air Fryer Shrimp Scampi

Prep Time: 5 mins; Cook Time: 10 mins;Total Time: 15 mins.

Yield: 4 Servings.

INGREDIENTS
- ❖ 4 tablespoons Butter
- ❖ 1 tablespoon lemon juice
- ❖ 1 tablespoon Minced Garlic
- ❖ 2 teaspoons Red Pepper Flakes
- ❖ 1 tablespoon chopped chives
- ❖ 1 tablespoon minced basil leaves, plus more for sprinkling
- ❖ 2 tablespoons Chicken Stock
- ❖ 1 pound defrosted shrimp

INSTRUCTIONS
1. Preheat your air fryer to 3250C and Place a 6 x 3 metal pan in it to heat.
2. Place the butter, garlic, and red pepper flakes into the hot 6-inch pan.
3. Allow it to cook for 2 minutes, stirring once, until the butter has melted.
4. Open the air fryer, add all other ingredients to the pan, stirring gently.
5. Allow shrimp to cook for 5 minutes, stirring once. At this point, the butter should be well-melted and liquid, bathing the shrimp in spiced goodness.
6. Mix very well, remove the 6-inch pan using silicone mitts, and let it rest for 1 minute on the counter.
7. Stir after a minute.
8. Sprinkle additional fresh basil leaves and enjoy.

NUTRITIONAL FACTS (Per Serving)

- ✓ 220 calories; 23g protein; 1g carbs 13g fat.

Air Fried Chicken Nuggets Recipe

Prep Time: 10 mins; Cook Time: 8 mins; Total Time: 18 mins.

Yield: 4 Servings.

INGREDIENTS

- ❖ 1 boneless skinless chicken breast
- ❖ 1/4 teaspoon salt
- ❖ 1/8 teaspoon black pepper
- ❖ 1/2 cup unsalted butter melted
- ❖ 1/2 cup breadcrumbs
- ❖ 2 tablespoons grated Parmesan (optional)

INSTRUCTIONS

1. Preheat air fryer to 4000F for 4 minutes.
2. Trim any fat from chicken breast, Slice into 1/2 inch thick slices, then each slice into 2 to 3 nuggets. Season chicken pieces with salt and pepper.
3. Place melted butter in a small bowl and breadcrumbs (with Parmesan, if using) in another small bowl.
4. Dip each piece of chicken in butter, then breadcrumbs.
5. Place in a single layer in the air fryer basket and air fry for 8 minutes the temperature of chicken nuggets is at least 165 degrees F.
6. Transfer nuggets with tongs to a serving plate to cool.
7. Serve with fruit salad and yogurt if you desire.
8. Enjoy!

NUTRITIONAL FACTS (Per Serving)

- ✓ 123 calories; 16g fat; 3g net carbs; 12g protein.

Air Fryer Chips

Prep Time: 30 mins; Cook Time: 30 mins; Total Time: 1 hour.
Yield: 2 Servings.

INGREDIENTS

- 2 Large Red Potatoes, peeled and thinly sliced
- 2 teaspoons salt
- 4 garlic cloves crushed or minced
- 2 tablespoons homemade vegan parmesan

INSTRUCTIONS

1. Place the sliced potatoes in a bowl and fill with water.
2. Add 2 teaspoons of salt and let soak for 30 minutes.
3. Drain and rinse the potatoes. Pat dry.
4. Toss the potatoes with crushed garlic and vegan parmesan.
5. Layer half of the potato slices in the air fryer, in 4 layers.
6. Preheat air fryer to 350F.
7. Fry in the air fryer for 20-25 minutes, or until dry to the touch and no longer flimsy. Stir and toss the basket every 5 minutes.
8. Increase the heat to 4000C and air fry for an additional 5 minutes or until the potatoes have become crunchy.
9. Remove from the air fryer and top with more parmesan and season with more salt if needed.
10. Repeat for the other half of the potato slices.
11. Enjoy your chips!

NUTRITIONAL FACTS (Per Serving)

- 62 calories; 4g fat; 3g net carbs; 3g protein.

Air Fried Walnuts Loaf Recipe

Prep Time: 37 mins; Cook Time: 18 mins; Total Time: 55 mins.
Yield: 4 Servings.

INGREDIENTS

- 1/2 cup whole wheat flour
- 1/2 coarse-chopped walnuts

- ❖ 1 cup plain flour
- ❖ 7g instant yeast
- ❖ 2/3 teaspoon kosher salt
- ❖ 1 cup lukewarm water

INSTRUCTIONS

1. In a mixing bowl, combine all the flour with salt and mix. Add the yeast and walnuts and stir. While stirring, add water and mix until the dough forms a softball.
2. Knead the dough until it becomes smooth and elastic. Then shape it into a ball and place in a bowl covered with a plastic wrap. Place in a warm place to rise for about 30 minutes.
3. Preheat your air fryer to 400°F. Brush the top of the bread with some water. Place it in a small cake pan that fits into your air fryer and put the pan in the fryer basket. Set the timer to 18 minutes and air fry the dough until golden brown and well cooked. Allow the bread to cool on a wire rack.
4. ENJOY!

NUTRITIONAL FACTS (Per Serving)

✓ **62 calories; 7g fat; 4g net carbs; 3g protein.**

Air Fryer Bacon

Prep Time: 2 mins; Cook Time: 10 mins; Total Time: 12 mins.

Yield: 8 Servings.

INGREDIENT

- ❖ 2 ounces bacon or to taste

INSTRUCTIONS

1. Place a single layer of bacon in the air fryer basket.
2. Set the air fryer to 3250F and cook for 10 minutes.
3. Check for crispness and cook 2 more minutes if needed.
4. Drain bacon between batches to remove excess fat.

NUTRITIONAL FACTS (Per Serving)

✓ **138 calories; 4g protein; 13g fat; 1g carbs.**

Air Fried Salmon

Prep Time: 7 mins; Cook Time: 8 mins Total; Time: 15 mins.

Yield: 2 people.

INGREDIENTS
- 2 wild-caught salmon fillets (1-1/12-inches thick)
- 2 teaspoons avocado oil or olive oil
- 2 teaspoons paprika
- Salt and coarse black pepper, to taste
- lemon wedges

INSTRUCTIONS
1. Preheat air fryer to 4000F.
2. Remove any bones from the fillets and let the fillets sit on the counter for at about 1 hour.
3. Rub each fillet with olive oil.
4. Add paprika, and generously season with salt and pepper.
5. Place fillets in the air fryer basket and cook for 7-8 minutes or to taste.
6. Serve and enjoy.

NUTRITIONAL FACTS (Per Serving)
- 288 calories; 19g fat; 1g net carbs; 28g protein.

Air Fryer Mexican Street Corn Recipe

Prep Time: 5 mins; Cook Time: 15 mins; Total Time: 20 mins.

Yield: 4 Pieces of Corn.

INGREDIENTS
- 4 pieces of fresh corn on the cob cleaned
- 1/4 cup crumbled cotija cheese or Feta cheese
- 1/4 teaspoon chili powder
- 1/2 teaspoon Stone House Seasoning (you can use your preferred seasoning)
- 1/4 cup chopped fresh cilantro
- 1 medium lime cut into wedges

INSTRUCTIONS

1. Heat air fryer to 400°F.
2. Place corn into the air fryer basket and cook at for 10 minutes.
3. Sprinkle corn with cheese and cook for 5 more minutes.
4. Remove from air fryer and sprinkle with chili powder, Stone House Seasoning, and cilantro.
5. Serve with lime wedges.

NUTRITIONAL FACTS (Per Serving)

- ✓ 102 calories; 3g fat; 16g net carbs; 4g protein.

Air Fryer Chicken Sandwich

Prep Time: 10 mins; Cook Time: 16 mins; Total Time: 26 mins.

Yield: 6 Sandwiches.

INGREDIENTS

- 2 chicken boneless breasts, skinless (pounded, 1/2 inch thick)
- 1/2 cup milk
- 1/2 cup dill pickle juice
- 2 eggs
- 1 cup all-purpose flour
- 2 tablespoons powdered sugar
- 2 tablespoons potato starch
- 1 teaspoon paprika
- 1 teaspoon sea salt
- 1 oil mister
- 1/2 teaspoon freshly ground black pepper
- 1/2 teaspoon Garlic Powder
- 1/4 teaspoon ground celery seed ground
- 8 dill pickle chips
- 1 tablespoon extra virgin olive oil
- 4 hamburger buns toasted and buttered
- 1/4 teaspoon cayenne pepper, optional
- Mayonnaise, to serve (optional)

INSTRUCTIONS

1. Preheat air fryer to 3400F. Divide chicken pieces into two parts.
2. Place the chicken into Ziploc bag and pour in pickle juice. Marinate in the refrigerator for at least 30 minutes. In a medium bowl, beat egg with the milk. In another bowl, combine flour, starch, and all spices.
3. Using tongs, coat chicken evenly with egg mixture and then into the flour mixture. Shake off excess flour. Spray the basket of your air fryer with Oil.
4. Place chicken in air fryer and spray the chicken with oil and cook for 6 minutes.
5. Flip the chicken, spray with oil and cook for 6 more minutes. Raise the temperature to 400F and cook for 2 minutes on each side. Serve on buttered and toasted buns, with 2 pickle chips and a small dollop of mayonnaise, if using.

NUTRITIONAL FACTS (Per Sandwich)

✓ **281 calories; 6g fat; 38g carbs; 1g fiber; 15g protein.**

Air Fryer Chicken Burritos

Prep Time: 5 mins; Cook Time: 5 mins; Total Time: 10 mins.

Yield: 4 Rolls.

INGREDIENTS

- 1 cup shredded rotisserie chicken
- 4 small 6" tortilla
- 1/2 cup cream cheese
- 1/2 cup salsa
- 1/2 cup shredded cheese
- 1/4 cup salsa
- 1/4 cup sour cream

INSTRUCTIONS

1. Preheat air fryer to 3500F
2. Lay out the tortilla
3. Spread 2 tablespoons cream cheese across the entire tortilla
4. Spread out 2 tablespoons salsa across 2/3 of tortilla (do not spread on the edge of the cream cheese)
5. Spread out 1-2 tablespoons chicken on salsa
6. Top with 1 1/2 tablespoons shredded cheese

7. Roll tortilla and use cream cheese as a glue to seal the burrito
8. Spritz with cooking spray
9. Air fry for 5 minutes
10. While rolls are air frying, mix together salsa & sour cream for dipping sauce.
11. Serve and enjoy!

NUTRITIONAL FACTS (Per Serving)

- ✓ 138 calories; 4g protein; 13g fat; 2g carbs.

Air Fryer Nachos

Prep Time: 10 mins; Cook Time: 5 mins; Total Time: 15 mins.

Yield: 6 servings.

INGREDIENTS
- ❖ Grilled chicken
- ❖ Black beans, drained and rinsed
- ❖ White Queso
- ❖ Tortilla chips
- ❖ 1/2 cup grape tomatoes, halved
- ❖ 1/4 cup yellow or green onion, thinly sliced

INSTRUCTIONS
1. Line the basket of the air fryer with foil.
2. Spray with non-stick spray.
3. Build the nachos, add the chips, chicken, and beans.
4. Add a layer of queso.
5. Top with tomatoes and onions.
6. Turn the air fryer to 1790C for 5 minutes or until crispy.
7. Enjoy!

NUTRITIONAL FACTS (Per Servings)

- ✓ 130 calories; 4g protein; 13g fat; 1g carbs.

Air Fryer Fried Catfish Recipe

Prep Time: 5 mins; Cook Time: 60 mins; Total Time: 65 mins.

Yield: 4 Servings.

INGREDIENTS
- 4 catfish fillets
- 1/4 cup fish fry seasoning
- 1 tablespoon olive oil
- 1 tablespoon chopped parsley, optional

INSTRUCTIONS
1. Preheat Air Fryer to 4000C.
2. Rinse the catfish and pat dry.
3. Pour the fish fry seasoning in a large Ziploc bag.
4. Add the catfish to the bag, one at a time.
5. Seal the bag and shake until the filets are evenly coated with seasoning.
6. Spray olive oil on each filet.
7. Working in batches, place the filets (1 or 2) in the air fryer basket and cook for 10 minutes.
8. Flip the fish. Cook for another 10 minutes, flip again and cook for 2 more minutes or until crispy.
9. Repeat for the remaining fillets.
10. When done, remove from air fryer and top with parsley.
11. Serve and enjoy.

NUTRITIONAL FACTS (Per Servings)
- 138 calories; 3g carbs ; 16g protein; 16g fat.

Air Fried Ham & Egg Toast Cup

Prep Time: 10 mins; Cook Time: 15 mins; Total Time: 25 mins.

Yield: 4 Servings.

INGREDIENTS
- 4 ramekins
- 4 eggs
- 8 slices of whole-meal toast

- ❖ 2 Slices of Ham (your preferred ham)
- ❖ Butter
- ❖ Pinch of salt more to taste
- ❖ Pinch of pepper
- ❖ 1 slice cheese, cut into small pieces (optional)

INSTRUCTIONS

1. Brush the interior of the ramekin with a sufficient amount of butter.
2. Flatten 8 slices of toast using your palms
3. Line the inside of each ramekin with a slice of flattened toast, making sure any extra folds are flattened and added.
4. Place another slice of flattened toast on top of each toast.
5. Cut 2 slices of ham into 8 smaller strips.
6. Line 2 strips of ham in each ramekin.
7. Crack an egg into each toast cup
8. Season each cup with salt and some ground black pepper.
9. Add some cheese into the toast cup (if using).
10. Place the ramekins into the Air fryer and air fry for 15 mins at 710C.
11. Once done, remove ramekins from the air fryer.
12. Remove toast cup from the ramekins, with a knife, slowly slice each round the inside of the ramekin and then wriggle with the same small knife and a spoon.
13. Serve and enjoy!

NUTRITIONAL FACTS (Per Servings)

- ✓ 69 calories; 2g carbs ; 16g protein; 13g fat.

Air fryer Beetroot Chips

Prep Time: 10 mins; Cook Time: 25 mins; Total Time: 35 mins.

Yield: 2 Servings.

INGREDIENTS

- ❖ 2 medium-sized beetroot
- ❖ 1/2 teaspoon olive Oil
- ❖ Salt to taste
- ❖ Pepper to taste, optional

INSTRUCTIONS

1. Wash the Beetroot, peel the skin and set the skin aside.
2. Using a mandoline slicer, slice them thin.
3. Use the skin to dye your prop if you want to or just put it into your food waste.
4. Spread the beetroot slices on the paper and place another paper on top of it. Let it sit for 10 minutes.
5. Toss the sliced beetroot in oil and sprinkle with salt
6. Preheat the air fryer to 149F for 4 minutes.
7. Place the chips in the air fryer basket and cook for 15 minutes, shaking every 5 minutes.
8. Once the chips are slightly crisp on the outer edges and tender in the middle, allow them to cool down for some time.
9. Place back into the air fryer, increase heat to 820C air fryer for another 3 minutes.
10. Serve warm and enjoy.

NUTRITIONAL FACTS (Per Servings)

✓ **108 calories; 3g carbs ; 13g protein; 17g fat.**

Air Fried Coconut Shrimp with Marmalade Sauce

Prep Time: 10 mins; Cook Time: 20 mins; Total Time: 30 mins.

Yield: 2 Servings.

INGREDIENTS

- 8 large shrimp, shell removed, and deveined
- 1/2 cup breadcrumb
- 8 ounces coconut milk
- 1/2 cup shredded sweetened coconut
- 1/2 teaspoon cayenner pepper
- 1/4 teaspoon kosher salt
- 1/4 teaspoon fresh ground pepper
- 1/2 cup orange marmalade
- 1 tablespoon honey
- 1 teaspoon mustard
- 1/4 teaspoon hot sauce

INSTRUCTIONS

1. Clean the shrimp and set aside.
2. In a small bowl, whisk the coconut milk and season with salt and pepper. Set aside. In a separate small bowl, whisk together the coconut, breadcrumb, cayenne pepper, salt, and pepper.
3. One at a time, dip the shrimp in the coconut milk, the breadcrumb and then place in the basket of the fryer. Repeat for the remaining shrimp.
4. Cook the shrimp in the fryer for 20 minutes at 1760C or until shrimp are cooked through.
5. Meanwhile, whisk together the marmalade, honey, mustard, and hot sauce.
6. Serve the shrimp with the sauce and enjoy.

NUTRITIONAL FACTS (Per Servings)

- ✓ **138 calories; 5g carbs ; 18g protein; 16g fat.**

Air Fryer Spicy Chicken Thighs

Prep Time: 10 mins; Cook Time: 55 mins; Total Time: 1 hour 5 mins.

Yields: 4 servings.

INGREDIENTS

- ❖ 1/3 cup low-sodium soy sauce
- ❖ 1/4 cup extra-virgin olive oil
- ❖ 2 tablespoons honey
- ❖ 2 tablespoons chili garlic sauce
- ❖ Juice of 1 lime
- ❖ 2 cloves garlic, minced
- ❖ 2 teaspoons freshly grated ginger
- ❖ 4 bone-in chicken thighs, skin-on (2 pounds)
- ❖ Thinly sliced green onions, for garnish
- ❖ Toasted sesame seeds, for garnish

INSTRUCTIONS

1. In a large bowl, combine soy sauce, oil, honey, chili garlic sauce, lime juice, garlic, and ginger. Reserve ½ cup of marinade. Add chicken thighs to the bowl and toss to coat. Cover and refrigerate for at least 30 minutes.

2. Remove 2 thighs from marinade and place in the basket of your air fryer. Cook at 400° until thighs are cooked through to an internal temperature of 165°, about 15-20 minutes. Transfer thighs to a plate and tent with foil. Repeat with remaining thighs.
3. Meanwhile, in a small saucepan over medium heat, bring reserved marinade to a boil. Reduce heat and simmer until sauce thickens slightly 4 to 5 minutes.
4. Brush sauce over thighs and garnish with green onions and sesame seeds before serving.
5. Serve and enjoy!

NUTRITIONAL FACTS (Per Servings)
- ✓ 150 calories; 3g carbs ; 18g protein; 19.5g fat.

Gluten-free Air Fried Jalapeno Poppers

Prep Time: 7 mins; Cook Time: 8 mins; Total Time: 15 mins.

Yield: 2 Servings.

INGREDIENTS
- ❖ 10 jalapenopeppers halved and deseeded
- ❖ 8 oz of cream cheese I used a dairy-freecream cheese
- ❖ 1/4 cup fresh parsley
- ❖ 3/4 cup gluten-free bread crumbs

INSTRUCTIONS
1. Preheat air fryer to 375°F
2. Mix together 1/2 of crumbs and cream cheese. Once combined add in the parsley.
3. Stuff each pepper with the mixture.
4. Gently press the tops of the peppers into the remaining 1/4 c of crumbs to create the top coating.
5. Cook in an air fryer 8 minutes.
6. Let cool for some minutes.
7. Serve and enjoy.

NUTRITIONAL FACTS (Per Servings)
- ✓ 65 calories; 3g carbs ; 5g protein; 6g fat.

Air Fried Fish Finger Sandwich

Prep Time: 5 mins; Cook Time: 15 mins; Total Time: 20 mins.

Yield: 4 Servings.

INGREDIENTS

- 4 small skinless cod fillets
- 40g dried breadcrumbs
- 2 tablespoons flour
- spray oil
- 250g frozen peas
- 1 tablespoon Greek yogurt
- 10 capers
- Pepper to taste
- A squeeze of lemon juice
- 4 bread rolls
- Sea salt to taste
- Lettuce, optional topping

INSTRUCTIONS

1. Preheat your air fryer to 400^0F
2. Season each fillet with salt and pepper and lightly coat with the flour.
3. Then roll quickly in the breadcrumbs.
4. Spray the fryer basket and Place the fillets on top and cook on the fish for 15 mins.
5. Meanwhile, cook the peas in boiling water for some minutes on in the microwave. Drain and then add to a blender with the creme fraiche, capers and lemon juice to taste. Blitz until combined.
6. Once the fish has cooked, remove it from the fryer.
7. Layer sandwich with the bread, fish and pea puree. Top with lettuce (if using)
8. Serve with tartar sauce if desired, and enjoy.

NUTRITIONAL FACTS (Per Servings)

- ✓ 138 calories; 3g carbs ; 18.5g protein; 18g fat.

Air Fried Taco Bell Crunch Wrap

Prep Time: 15 mins; Cook Time: 5 mins; Total Time: 20 mins.

Yield: 6 Servings.

INGREDIENTS

- 2 pounds ground beef
- 2 servings Taco Seasoning
- 1 1/3 cup water
- 6 (12 inches) flour tortillas
- 3 roma tomatoes
- 12 ounces nacho cheese
- 2 cup lettuce, shredded
- 2 cup Mexican blend cheese
- 2 cup sour cream
- 6 tostadas
- Olive oil

INSTRUCTIONS

1. Preheat air fryer to 400^0F
2. Prepare ground beef according to taco seasoning packet
3. Stuff the center of each flour tortilla with 2/3 cup of beef, 4 tablespoons of nacho cheese, 1 tostada, 1/3 cup sour cream, 1/3 cup lettuce, 1/6th of the tomatoes and 1/3 cup cheese
4. To close, flood the edges up, over the center.
5. Repeat 2 and 3 with remaining wraps
6. Lay seam side down in your air fryer
7. Spray with oil
8. Cook for 2-3 minutes or until brown
9. Using a spatula, carefully flip and spray again, and cook 2 more minutes.
10. Repeat with remaining wraps
11. Allow to cool a few minutes and enjoy.

NUTRITIONAL FACTS (Per Servings)

- ✓ **182 calories; 16g fat ; 3g carbs ; 13g protein.**

Air Fryer Roasted Black pepper Pork Ribs

Prep Time: 5 mins; Cook Time: 35 mins; Total Time: 40 mins.

Yield: 2 Servings.

INGREDIENTS

- 1 rack of ribs
- 1 1/2 tablespoon spice mixture
- 1 tablespoon vegetable oil
- 2 tablespoons black pepper sauce.

INSTRUCTIONS

1. Place meat in a shallow bowl, add oil, spice mixture, and black pepper sauce and mix well so that the meat is coated. (Be sure to reserve 1-2 teaspoons of sauce for garnish). Pour mixture into a ziplock bag and refrigerate for at least 1 hour.
2. Preheat air fryer to 248F.
3. Place ribs in the air fryer basket and cook for 30 minutes.
4. Then increase the heat to 400F and air fry for 5 more minutes.
5. Remove from the air fryer, cover the meat in aluminum foil and allow it to cool for 5-10 minutes.
6. After cooling, spread reserved sauce over the meat and serve.

NUTRITIONAL FACTS (Per Servings)

- ✓ 182 calories; 16g fat ; 3g carbs ; 13g protein.

Air Fried Bow Tie Pasta Chips

Prep Time: 30 mins; Cook Time: 10 mins; Total Time: 40 mins.

Yield: 2 Servings.

INGREDIENTS

- 1 tablespoon olive oil
- 1 tablespoon nutritional yeast
- 2 cups 152g dry whole wheat bow tie pasta
- 1 1/2 teaspoons Italian Seasoning Blend
- 1/2 teaspoon salt

INSTRUCTIONS

1. Cook the pasta for half the time called for on the package. Toss the drained pasta with the olive oil, nutritional yeast, Italian seasoning, and salt.
2. Meanwhile, preheat air fryer to 200°C.
3. Place the mixture in your air fryer basket.
4. Cook for 5 minutes. Shake the basket and cook 4 minutes more or until crunchy.
5. Serve and enjoy!

NUTRITIONAL FACTS (Per Serving)

✓ 294 calories; 10g protein; 45g carbs; 8g fat.

Air Fried Sweet-Sour Pork

Prep Time: 15 mins; Cook Time: 30 mins; Total Time: 45 mins.

Yield: 4 Servings.

INGREDIENTS

- 300g pork (sweet and sour pork)
- 2 dashes Maggi seasoning
- 1 teaspoon soy sauce
- Dash of sesame oil
- Ground pepper to taste
- A slice of pineapple, cut in cubes
- I teaspoon garlic, minced
- 2 tablespoons oyster sauce
- 1 tomato, cubed
- I large egg
- 1 tablespoon tomato sauce
- 1 onion, finely sliced
- 1 tablespoon Worcester sauce
- Sugar to taste
- Plain flour

INSTRUCTIONS

1. Cut the pork into cube sizes and place in a shallow bowl. Add the next four ingredients and combine. Pour mixture into a ziplock bag and put in the fridge for 1-2 hours.

2. Heat up your air fryer to 120C for 4-5 mins.
3. Dip pork in egg and coat with flour.
4. Dust off any excess flour on the pork and place it in your air fryer basket.
5. Cook for 20 minutes. Set aside.
6. Prepare the sauce as follows:
7. Fry garlic and onion for 1 minute in 1 teaspoon of oil. Add tomatoes and pineapple.
8. Add all the sauces and stir
9. Add the pork mixture and coat well with the sauce
10. Add sugar and enjoy!

NUTRITIONAL FACTS (Per Servings)
- ✓ 182 calories; 21g fat ; 3g carbs ; 13g protein.

Air Fryer Vegan Stuffed Potatoes

Prep Time: 10 mins; Cook Time: 1 hour 10 mins; Total Time: 1 hour 20 mins.

Yield: 4 Servings.

INGREDIENTS
- ❖ 2 large Potatoes
- ❖ 2 teaspoons olive oil
- ❖ 1/4 cup unsweetened vegan yogurt
- ❖ 1/4 cup unsweetened nondairy milk
- ❖ 2 tablespoons nutritional yeast
- ❖ 1/2 teaspoon salt
- ❖ 1/4 teaspoon pepper
- ❖ 1 cup chopped spinach
- ❖ Chopped chives

INSTRUCTIONS
1. Rub each potato with oil on all sides.
2. Preheat your air fryer to 400°F.
3. Add the potatoes to your air fryer basket and air fry for 30 minutes, then turn the potatoes over and cook for 30 more minutes.
4. Let the potatoes cool enough that you can touch them without burning yourself.

5. Cut each potato in half lengthwise and carefully scoop out the middle of the potato while leaving enough to create a stable shell of the potato skin and a thin layer of the white part.
6. Mash the scooped potato, vegan yogurt, nondairy milk, nutritional yeast, salt, and pepper until smooth.
7. Stir in the chopped spinach and fill the potato shells with the mixture.
8. Cook on 356F for 5 minutes.
9. Serve with chives.

NUTRITIONAL FACTS (Per Servings)
✓ 182 calories; 9g fat ; 19g carbs ; 11g protein.

Air Fried Tofu Rancheros

Prep Time: 10 mins; Cook Time: 25 mins; Total Time: 35 mins.

Yield: 4 Servings.

INGREDIENTS
Spice Crusted Tofu
- 1 - 20 ounces container High Protein Tofu, cut into cubes
- 1 teaspoon ground cumin powder
- 1 teaspoon ground chili powder
- 1/2 teaspoon smoked paprika
- 1/4 teaspoon salt

Salsa Beans
- 1 (15 1/2 ounce) can organic black beans, drained.
- 1/4 cup Little Face Big Taste Jalapeno Cilantro Salsa or your fav mild salsa
- 1/8 to 1/4 teaspoon liquid smoke to suit your taste
- 1/8 teaspoon jalapeno powder
- 1/8 teaspoon cumin powder
- Salt to taste

Toppings
- 1/3 cup grated carrot
- 1/3 cup grated zucchini
- 1/3 cup grated yellow squash
- 1/8 teaspoon salt
- pinch black pepper

The Base
- 4 large flour or gluten-free tortillas I used Ezekiel brand
- 1 cup shredded vegan cheese

INSTRUCTIONS

Make the Spice Crusted Tofu

1. In a shallow bowl, combine the tofu cubes with the cumin, chili powder, smoked paprika, and salt.
2. Preheat the air fryer to 400°F.
3. Once it's hot, add the coated tofu to your air fryer basket and cook for 5 minutes and when the time is up, shake the tofu. Repeat for an additional 5 minutes.
4. Make the Salsa Beans
5. Mix all the ingredients together in a small bowl.
6. Prepare the Base
7. Take 2 tortillas and put on a baking sheet while preheating the oven to 176C. Spread 1/4 cup vegan cheese on top of each tortilla. Put 1/4 of the salsa beans in the middle of the tortilla and bake for 15 minutes.
8. Once warm add on the Spiced Crusted Tofu, the shredded veggie topping, chopped tomatoes or other veggies you'd like to pile on like avocado or shredded lettuce.
9. Top with Salsa and enjoy.

NUTRITIONAL FACTS (Per Servings)
- 151 calories; 16g fat ; 3g carbs ; 13g protein.

Air Fried Eggless Chocolate Chip Muffins

Prep Time: 10 mins; Cook Time: 10 mins; Total Time: 20 mins.

Yield: 6 Servings.

INGREDIENTS
- 1/2 cup plain flour
- 1/2 cup baking powder
- 1/2 teaspoon salt
- 1 teaspoon apple cider vinegar
- 1 tablespoon cocoa powder
- 1/4 teaspoon baking soda
- 1/4 cup sugar

- 1 tablespoon honey
- 2 tablespoons yogurt
- 4 tablespoons milk
- 2 tablespoons coconut oil
- 1/2 teaspoon vanilla extract
- 2 tablespoons chocolate chips

INSTRUCTIONS

1. Preheat air fryer at 400F.
2. Remove 1 tablespoon flour from the 1/2 cup flour and add 1 tablespoon cocoa powder. Add baking powder and salt. Add baking soda, sugar and combine with a fork.
3. In a small bowl, whisk together milk, yogurt, oil and vanilla extract until combined.
4. Make a well in the dry ingredients and add the wet ingredients. Add the vinegar.
5. Stir to combine. Mix in the chocolate chips.
6. Spoon the mix into 6 silicone muffin moulds
7. Place 4 at a time in the wire basket of the preheated air fryer.
8. Cook in the air fryer for 8 minutes, after which you can insert a skewer to see if it comes out clean, then, air fry the remaining.
9. Remove and cool for 5 minutes. Remove from moulds and serve.

NUTRITIONAL FACTS (Per Servings)

✓ **109 calories; 6g fat ; 2g carbs ; 6g protein.**

Vegan Air Fried Carrot Cake

Prep Time: 10 mins; Cook Time: 15 mins; Total Time: 25 mins.

Yield: 1 Serving.

INGREDIENTS

- 1/4 cup whole wheat pastry flour, or gluten-free baking mix to make gluten-free
- 1 tablespoon coconut sugar
- 1/4 teaspoon baking powder
- 1/4 teaspoon ground cinnamon
- 1/8 teaspoon ground dried ginger
- pinch ground allspice
- pinch ground cloves
- 2 tablespoons unsweetened nondairy milk plus

- ❖ 2 teaspoons unsweetened nondairy milk
- ❖ 2 tablespoons grated carrot
- ❖ 2 tablespoons chopped walnuts
- ❖ 1 tablespoon chopped dates
- ❖ 2 teaspoons mild oil

INSTRUCTIONS

1. Oil an air fryer-safe mug/ baking pan.
2. Add the flour, sugar, baking powder, cinnamon, ginger, allspice, and salt then mix well with a fork.
3. Add milk, carrot, walnuts, dates, and oil and mix again.
4. Cook at 356 F for 15 minutes. Check with a fork to make sure the middle is cooked. If not, cook for an additional 5 minutes.

NUTRITIONAL FACTS (Per Serving)

- ✓ 310 calories; 8g protein; 22g fat; 46g carbs

Air Fried Blueberriesand Apple Crumble

Prep Time: 15 mins; Cook Time: 15 mins; Total Time: 30 mins.

Yield: 2 Servings.

INGREDIENTS

- ❖ 1 medium apple finely diced
- ❖ 2 tablespoons non-dairy butter
- ❖ 1/2 cup frozen blueberries
- ❖ 1/4 cup plus 1 tablespoon brown rice flour (reserve some for sprinkling).
- ❖ 2 tablespoons sugar
- ❖ 1/2 teaspoon ground cinnamon

INSTRUCTIONS

1. Preheat the air fryer to 356°F.
2. In a ramekin, combine the apple and blueberries.
3. Combine the flour, sugar, cinnamon, and butter in a small bowl.
4. Spoon the flour mixture over the fruit.
5. Sprinkle a little extra flour over everything to cover any exposed fruit and air fry for 15 minutes.

NUTRITIONAL FACTS(Per Serving)
- ✓ 309 calories; 2g protein;50g carbs; 5g fiber; 26g sugar; 12g fats.

Air Fried Seitan Vegan Riblets with Mushroom

Prep Time: 15 mins; Cook Time: 20 mins; Total Time: 35 mins.

Yield: 4 Servings.

INGREDIENTS
- ❖ 1 teaspoon mushroom powder
- ❖ 1 cup vital wheat gluten
- ❖ 1/4 cup nutritional yeast
- ❖ 1 teaspoon onion powder
- ❖ 1/2 teaspoon garlic powder
- ❖ 3/4 cup water
- ❖ 1/4 cup BBQ sauce
- ❖ 1 teaspoon salt, optional

INSTRUCTIONS
1. Add the wheat, yeast, mushroom powder, onion powder, salt and garlic powder to your food processor.
2. Pulse until mixed well.
3. Let the dough settle, then drizzle the water in through the top opening while you have the processor on.
4. Then let the food processor run for about 3 minutes more to knead the seitan.
5. Remove dough and put it on a cutting board and knead a little bit more with your hands.
6. Press and pull the dough to the shape of your air fryer basket, then cut in half.
7. Place the halves into your air fryer and cook on 370°F for 8 minutes. Then flip over and cook 5 more minutes.
8. Slice half of the seitan into 1/2-inch wide strips, then toss with about 1/4 cup of your favorite BBQ sauce. Place in an oven-safe container that fits into your air fryer and cook at 370°F for 5 minutes.

NUTRITIONAL FACTS (Per Serving)
- ✓ **272 calories; 19g carbs; 3g fiber; 2g fat; 47g protein.**

Air Fried Pecan-Crusted Gardein Fishless Filets

Prep Time: 5 mins; Cook Time: 15 mins; Total Time: 20 mins.

Yield: 3 Servings.

INGREDIENTS
- 3/4 cup minced pecans
- 1 10.1 ounces Package Gardein Golden Fishless Filets (frozen)
- 1/4 cup plus 2 tablespoons finely ground cornmeal
- 3 tablespoons ground flax seed
- 1 teaspoon Cajun seasoning blend
- 3/4 cup water

INSTRUCTIONS
1. Remove the package of Gardein Golden Fishless Filets from the freezer while you prepare the coating.
2. Mix the pecans, cornmeal, flaxseed, water, and Cajun seasoning blend in a small bowl that will fit a whole fillet. Once mixed together it will be a very thick batter.
3. Using your hands, press the coating on the top and bottom of a filet, then as you flatten it with your palms cover the edges as well. Get a small bit of the batter as you need to cover the whole filet.
4. Once coated, place on a piece of parchment paper cut for your air fryer that leaves 1 inch around the inside of the basket for the air to flow through.
5. Repeat until the basket is full but not crowded. Cook at 390 F for 10 minutes. Flip and cook for 4 minutes more, or until the center is piping hot.

NUTRITIONAL FACTS (Per Serving (Serving Size Is 2 Filets)
- ✓ 310 calories; 12g protein; 5g net carbs; 27g fat.

Air Fryer Tofu with Orange Sauce

Prep Time: 15 mins; Cook Time: 25 mins; Total Time: 40 mins.

Yield: 4 Servings.

INGREDIENTS
- 1 pound super-firm tofu drained and pressed
- 1 tablespoon tamari
- 1 tablespoon cornstarch

- 1 teaspoon orange zest
- 1/3 cup orange juice
- 2 teaspoons cornstarch
- 1/4 teaspoon crushed red pepper flakes
- 1 teaspoon fresh ginger minced
- 1/2 cup water
- 1 tablespoon pure maple syrup
- 1 teaspoon fresh garlic minced

INSTRUCTIONS

1. Cut the tofu in cubes.
2. Place the tofu cubes in a ziplock bag, add tamari and seal the bag. Shake the bag until tofu is evenly coated.
3. Add the tablespoon of cornstarch to the bag and shake to coat. Set aside to marinate for at least 15 minutes.
4. Meanwhile, add all the sauce ingredients to a small bowl and mix with a spoon. Set aside.
5. Working in batches, place the tofu in the air fryer in a single layer.
6. Cook the tofu at 390 F for 10 minutes, shaking it after 5 minutes. Repeat for the other batch or batches.
7. When done cooking, add the tofu to a skillet over medium-high heat.
8. Stir sauce and pour it over the tofu. Stir the mixture until the sauce has thickened and the tofu is heated through.
9. Serve warm and enjoy!

NUTRITIONAL FACTS (Per Serving)

- 102 calories; 9g protein; 2g fat; 10g net carbs.

Air Fryer Caribbean Spiced Chicken

Prep Time: 10 mins; Cook Time: 10 mins; Total Time: 20 mins.

Yield: 8 Servings.

INGREDIENTS

- 3 pounds skinless chicken thigh fillets (bones removed)
- 1 tablespoon ground coriander seed
- 1 tablespoon ground cinnamon

- ❖ coarse ground black pepper to taste
- ❖ 1-1/2 teaspoons ground ginger
- ❖ 1-1/2 teaspoons ground nutmeg
- ❖ 3 tablespoons melted coconut oil
- ❖ 1 tablespoon cayenne pepper
- ❖ salt to taste

INSTRUCTIONS

1. Remove chicken from packaging and pat dry. Place on a large baking sheet covered with paper towels to soak up any residual liquid. Season both sides of the chicken with salt and pepper to taste and let sit for 30 minutes.
2. Combine coriander, cinnamon, cayenne in a small bowl and mix. Add ginger and nutmeg to the bowl and until well combined.
3. Coat each piece of chicken with the mixture and brush both sides with coconut oil.
4. Heat your air fryer to 390F
5. Carefully arrange four pieces of chicken into your air fryer basket and air fry for 10 minutes.
6. Remove chicken from the basket, cover tightly with foil and place in an oven-safe dish.
7. Keep warm in the oven until all chicken is done. Repeat for the remaining chicken.
8. When done, serve and enjoy.

NUTRITIONAL FACTS (Per Serving)

✓ **202 calories; 1g net carbs; 25g protein; 13.4g fat.**

Air Fried Sriracha Honey Chicken Wings

Prep Time: 10 mins; Cook Time: 20 mins; Total Time: 30 mins.

Yield; 2 Servings.

INGREDIENTS

- ❖ 1 pound chicken wings, tips removed and wings cut into drummettes and flats.
- ❖ 1/4 cup honey
- ❖ 2 tablespoons sriracha sauce
- ❖ 1 1/2 tablespoons soy sauce
- ❖ 1 tablespoon butter
- ❖ Juice of 1/2 lime
- ❖ Scallions for garnish

INSTRUCTIONS

1. Preheat the air fryer to 360 F.
2. Add the chicken wings to the air fryer basket, and cook for 30 minutes. Be sure to flip chicken every 7 minutes while air frying.
3. Meanwhile, in a small saucepan add all the sauce ingredients and boil for 3 minutes.
4. When the chicken cooked, toss in a bowl with the sauce until fully coated.
5. Garnish with scallions and serve.

NUTRITIONAL FACTS (Per Serving)

- ✓ 140 calories; 24g protein; 2g fat; 23g net carbs.

Coconut Shrimp with Marmalade Sauce

Prep Time: 10 mins; Cook Time: 20 mins; Total Time: 30 mins.

Yield: 2 Servings.

INGREDIENTS

- ❖ 8 large shrimp shelled and deveined
- ❖ 8 ounces of coconut milk
- ❖ 1/2 cup breadcrumbs
- ❖ 1/2 teaspoon cayenner pepper
- ❖ 1/4 teaspoon fresh ground pepper
- ❖ 1/2 cup shredded sweetened coconut
- ❖ 1/2 cup orange marmalade
- ❖ 1 tablespoon honey
- ❖ 1 teaspoon mustard
- ❖ 1/4 teaspoon hot sauce
- ❖ 1/4 teaspoon salt

INSTRUCTIONS

1. Clean the shrimp and set aside.
2. In a small bowl, whisk the coconut milk and season with salt and pepper. Set aside.
3. In a different small bowl, whisk together the coconut, breadcrumbs, cayenne pepper, salt, and pepper.
4. One at a time, dip the shrimp in the coconut milk, the breadcrumbs and then place in the basket of the fryer. Repeat until all the shrimp are coated.
5. Cook the shrimp in the fryer at 350 degrees for 20 minutes or until the shrimp are cooked through.

6. Meanwhile, whisk together the marmalade, honey, mustard, and hot sauce.
7. Serve shrimp with the sauce and enjoy!.

NUTRITIONAL FACTS (Per Serving)

- ✓ 623 calories; 31g fat; 15g protein; 78g carbs; 1g fiber; 57g sugar.

Air fryer french fries

Prep Time: 5 mins; Cook Time: 20 mins;Total Time: 25 mins.

Yield: 2 Servings.

INGREDIENTS

- ❖ 3 medium potatoes
- ❖ 1 1/2 tablespoons olive oil
- ❖ Pepper to taste
- ❖ 1/4 teaspoon garlic powder
- ❖ salt to taste

INSTRUCTIONS

1. Peel the potatoes, wash and pat dry. Then slice.
2. Place sliced potatoes in a bowl and toss with oil, garlic, salt, and pepper.
3. Set your air fryer timing to 20 mins and cook on 400F, tossing potatoes around 2-3 times.
4. When done cooking, remove from the air fryer, allow to cool for 5 mins and serve.

NUTRITIONAL FACTS (Per Serving)

- ✓ 278 calories; 10g fat; 30g carbs; 7g protein.

Air Fryer Cauliflower Chickpea Tacos

Prep Time: 10 mins; Cook Time: 20 mins;Total Time: 30 mins.

Yield: 4 Servings.

INGREDIENTS

- ❖ 4 cups cauliflower florets cut into bite-sized pieces
- ❖ 19 oz can of chickpeas drained and rinsed
- ❖ 2 tablespoons olive oil

- ❖ 2 tablespoons taco seasoning
- ❖ 8 small tortillas
- ❖ 4 cups cabbage shredded
- ❖ 2 avocados sliced
- ❖ Coconut yogurt

INSTRUCTIONS

1. Pre-heat air fryer to 390°F.
2. In a large bowl, toss the cauliflower and chickpeas with olive oil and taco seasoning.
3. Place everything into the basket of your air fryer.
4. Cook in the air fryer, shaking the basket occasionally, for 20 minutes, or until cooked through. Cauliflower will be golden but not burnt.
5. Serve in tacos with avocado slices, cabbage, and coconut yogurt.
6. Enjoy!

NUTRITIONAL FACTS (Per Serving)

- ✓ 102 calories; 21g protein; 11g fat; 7g net carbs.

Air Fryer Coconut ShrimpWith Pina Colada Dip

Prep Time: 10 mins; Cook Time: 15 mins; Total Time: 25 mins.

Yield: 2 Servings.

INGREDIENTS

- ❖ 1 pound large shrimp
- ❖ 1/2 cup all-purpose flour
- ❖ 2 cups shredded sweetened coconut
- ❖ 1/2 teaspoon baking powder
- ❖ 1 teaspoon salt
- ❖ 2/3 cup water
- ❖ 1/2 cup panko

Pina Colada Dip

- ❖ 1 cup vanilla yogurt
- ❖ Zest of one lime
- ❖ 1/4 cup coconut
- ❖ 1 tablespoon dark rum

INSTRUCTIONS

Preheat your air fryer to 200F

1. Place the flour in a small bowl, add salt, water, and baking powder and whisk together. Set aside for 5 minutes.
2. In a separate bowl, mix panko and coconut together.
3. Dredge shrimp in liquid then coat in coconut mixture. Repeat for all other shrimp.
4. Working in batches, place shrimp in the air fryer basket and cook for 5 minutes.
5. Repeat for the remaining batch of shrimp.
6. To make pina colada dip, place all the ingredients in a small bowl. Mix together until well combined.
7. Serve coconut shrimp with pina colada dip and enjoy.

NUTRITIONAL FACTS (Per Serving)

- ✓ 186 calories; 24g carbs; 10g fat; 2g protein.

Air Fried Fish Sticks with Tartar Sauce

Prep Time: 10 mins; Cook Time: 20 mins; Total Ti,e: 40 mins.
Yield: 2 Servings.

INGREDIENTS

- ❖ 1 1/2 pounds cod
- ❖ 2 eggs
- ❖ 1 cup almond flour
- ❖ 1/2 cup tapioca starch
- ❖ 2 tablespoons avocado oil
- ❖ 1-1/2 teaspoon onion powder
- ❖ 1 teaspoon ground black pepper
- ❖ 1/2 teaspoon mustard powder
- ❖ 1-1/2 teaspoon dried dill
- ❖ 1 teaspoon sea salt
- ❖ Avocado Oil spray

Tartar Sauce

- ❖ 1 tablespoon chopped fresh parsley
- ❖ 1/3 cup avocado oil
- ❖ 1 tablespoon dill relish

- 1/4 teaspoon salt
- 2 teaspoons lemon juice

INSTRUCTIONS

1. Pre-heat air fryer to 390°F.
2. Pat fish dry and season with a pinch of salt and pepper.
3. Cut fish into very small fish sticks
4. Prepare two medium bowls. Place tapioca starch in the first, and whisk eggs in the second medium bowl.
5. In a large bowl, whisk almond flour, dill, onion powder, salt, pepper, and mustard powder.
6. Dip the sliced fish into the tapioca, shaking off any excess, then into the egg, then dredge in flour mixture. Repeat until all fish is coated.
7. Add the avocado oil to the basket and then spray the air fryer basket with avocado oil spray.
8. Arrange the fish sticks in the air fryer basket leaving space in between. Spray fish sticks with additional avocado spray to lightly coat and then cook for 11 minutes. Carefully flip after 5 minutes of air frying.
9. Repeat with remaining fish until they have all been cooked through to reach an internal temperature of 145°F.
10. While fish is cooking, make tartar sauce by combining all ingredients in a medium bowl. Set aside until fish is cooked.
11. Serve with tartar sauce and enjoy!

NUTRITIONAL FACTS (Per Serving)

- **186 calories; 5g carbs; 18g fat; 23g protein..**

Air Fried Thai Salmon Patties

Prep Time: 15 mins; Cook Time: 8 mins; Total Time: 23 mins.

Yield: 7 servings.

INGREDIENTS

- 14 ounces canned salmon, drained and bones removed
- 1/2 cup Panko breadcrumbs
- 1/4 teaspoon salt
- 1 1/2 tablespoon Thai red curry paste
- 1 1/2 tablespoons brown sugar

- ❖ zest from 1 lime
- ❖ 2 eggs
- ❖ spray oil

INSTRUCTIONS

1. Mix together all ingredients until red curry paste is evenly distributed through the salmon mixture.
2. Form mixture into 1/4 cup patties(1 inch thick and 2 inches across).
3. Heat air fryer to 360°F.
4. Spray patties with oil; flip and spray the other side.
5. Gently place patties into the air fryer basket; and, cooking in batches, air fry for 4 minutes, flip, then air fry for 4 more minutes.
6. Transfer to a plate and repeat with remaining patties until they are all cooked.
7. Serve and have fun!

NUTRITIONAL FACTS (Per Serving)

- ✓ **108 calories; 6g fat; 12g protein; 6g net carbs.**

Air Fryer Carrot Mug Cake

Prep Time: 15 mins; Cook Time: 20 mins; Total Time: 35 mins.

Yield: 1 Serving.

INGREDIENTS

- ❖ 1/4 cups whole wheat pastry flour
- ❖ 1 tablespoon brown sugar
- ❖ 1/4 teaspoon baking powder
- ❖ 1/4 teaspoon ground cinnamon
- ❖ 1/8 teaspoon ground dried ginger
- ❖ pinch ground allspice
- ❖ pinch salt
- ❖ 2 tablespoons plus 2 teaspoons non-dairy milk
- ❖ 2 tablespoons grated carrot
- ❖ 2 tablespoons chopped walnuts
- ❖ 1 tablespoons raisins or chopped dates
- ❖ 2 teaspoons mild oil

INSTRUCTIONS

1. Grease an oven-safe mug
2. Add the flour, sugar, baking powder, cinnamon, ginger, allspice, and salt then mix well with a fork until baking powder is evenly distributed.
3. Add the milk, carrot, walnuts, raisins, and oil then mix again. Cook at 350F for 15-20 minutes until cooked through in the middle.
4. Serve and enjoy.

NUTRITIONAL FACTS (Per Serving)

✓ 108 calories; 6g fat; 10g protein; 11g net carbs

Air Fried Brownies

Prep Time: 10 mins; Cook Time: 20 mins; Total Time: 30 mins.
Yield: 4 Servings.

INGREDIENTS

Wet Ingredients

- 1/4 cup nondairy milk
- 1/4 cup aquafaba
- 1/2 teaspoon vanilla extract

Dry Ingredients

- 1/4 cup cocoa powder
- 1/2 cup whole wheat pastry flour
- 1 tablespoon ground flax seeds
- 1/2 cup vegan sugar
- 1/4 teaspoon salt
- 1/4 cup chopped hazelnuts

INSTRUCTIONS

1. Mix the dry ingredients together in one bowl, and the wet ingredients in another bowl. Add the wet to the dry and mix well to combine.
2. Add the hazelnuts and mix again.
3. Preheat your air fryer to 350 F.
4. Spray some oil on a loaf pan and place the pan in your air fryer basket.
5. Cook for 20 minutes or until a knife can come out clean when stuck in the middle.
6. Serve and enjoy.

NUTRITIONAL FACTS (Per Serving)

- ✓ 108 calories; 8g fat; 9g protein; 10g net carbs

Air Fried Turkey Breast with Cherry Glaze

Prep Time: 10 mins; Cook Time: 55 min; Total Time: 1 hour 5 mins.
Yield 8 Servings.

INGREDIENTS

- ❖ 5 pounds bone-in turkey breast
- ❖ 1/2 cup cherry preserves
- ❖ 2 teaspoons olive oil
- ❖ 1 teaspoon dried thyme
- ❖ 1/4 teaspoon dried sage
- ❖ 1/2 teaspoon freshly ground black pepper
- ❖ 1 tablespoon chopped fresh thyme leaves
- ❖ 1 teaspoon soy sauce
- ❖ Freshly ground black pepper
- ❖ Fine sea salt to taste

INSTRUCTIONS

1. Preheat the air fryer to 350°F.
2. Brush the turkey breast all over with the olive oil. Combine the thyme, sage, salt, and pepper and rub the outside of the turkey breast with the spice mixture.
3. Transfer the seasoned turkey breast to the air fryer basket, breast side up, and air-fry at 350°F for 25 minutes. Turn the turkey breast on its side and air-fry for another 12 minutes. Turn the turkey breast on the opposite side and air-fry for another 12 minutes. The internal temperature of the turkey breast should reach 1650F when fully cooked.
4. While the turkey is cooking, combine the cherry preserves, fresh thyme, soy sauce and pepper in a small bowl. When the cooking time is up, return the turkey breast to an upright position and brush the glaze all over the turkey.
5. Air-fry for 5 minutes, until the skin is browned and crispy. Let the turkey rest before slicing.
6. Serve and enjoy.

NUTRITIONAL FACTS (Per Serving)

- ✓ 233 calories; 24g fat; 19g protein; 12g net carbs.

Air Fryer Buffalo Cauliflower

Prep Time: 5 mins; Cook Time: 15 mins; Total Time: 20 mins

Yield: 4 Servings

INGREDIENTS

For the Cauliflower

- 4 cups cauliflower florets.
- 1 cup panko breadcrumbs mixed with 1 teaspoon sea salt

For the Buffalo Coating

- 1/4 cup melted vegan butter
- 1/4 cup vegan buffalo sauce
- Salsa

INSTRUCTIONS

1. Melt the butter in a mug in the microwave, then whisk in the buffalo sauce.
2. Holding by the stem, dip each floret in the butter-buffalo mixture, to coat. Drain off any excess sauce.
3. Dredge the dipped floret in the panko/salt mixture, coating as much as you like, then place in the air fryer.
4. Air fry at 350F for 15 minutes, shaking a few times and checking their progress when you shake. Your cauliflower is done when the florets are a little bit browned.
5. Serve with salsa.

NUTRITIONAL FACTS (Per Serving)

- 140 calories; 18.5g fat; 19g protein; 6g net carbs

Air fried Kale Chips

Prep Time: 5 mins; Cook Time: 3 mins; Total Time: 8 mins

Yield: 1 Serving

INGREDIENTS

- 1 head of Kale
- 1 tablespoon of coconut oil
- 1 teaspoon of Soya Sauce

INSTRUCTIONS

1. Remove the center steam of the kale.
2. Tear the kale up into 1 1/2" pieces.
3. Wash clean and pat dry.
4. Toss with the oil and soya sauce.
5. Set your air fryer at 200 F for about 3 minutes. Toss once while air frying.
6. Serve and enjoy.

NUTRITIONAL FACTS (Per Serving)

- ✓ **95 calories; 6g fat; 7g protein; 7g net carbs.**

Air Fryer Turkey Fajitas Platter

Prep Time: 5 mins; Cook Time: 20 mins; Total Time: 25 mins

Yield: 2 Servings

INGREDIENTS

- 100 g leftover turkey breast
- 6 tortilla wraps
- 1 teaspoon Cumin
- 1 large yellow pepper
- 1 large avocado
- 1 large green pepper
- ½ small red onion, diced
- 5 tablespoons soft cheese
- 1 large red pepper
- 3 tablespoon cajun spice
- 2 tablespoons Mexican Seasoning
- Fine sea salt to taste
- Fresh coriander

INSTRUCTIONS

1. Slice the salad. Chop the avocado into little wedges, and thinly slice the peppers.
2. Chop turkey breast into small chunks.
3. Place the turkey, peppers, and onions into a bowl and mix with all the seasonings.
4. Place the turkey mixture in aluminum foil and arrange in your air fryer basket.
5. Set the air fryer on 392F and air fry for 20 minutes.

6. Take off heat when done, let cool for some minutes and serve with your favorite side dish.

NUTRITIONAL FACTS (Per Serving)

- ✓ 770 calories; 39g fat; 84g carbs; 21g fiber; 30g protein.

Air Fried Sweet Potato Cauliflower Patties with Ranch

Prep Time: 15 mins; Cook Time: 20 mins; otal Time: 35 mins.

Yield: 7 Servings.

INGREDIENTS

- 1 medium to large sweet potato, peeled
- 2 cups cauliflower florets
- 2 tablespoons organic ranch seasoning
- 1 green onion, chopped.
- 1 teaspoon minced garlic
- 1 cup packed fresh cilantro
- 1/4 teaspoon cumin
- 1/2 teaspoon chili powder
- 2 tablespoons arrowroot starch
- 1/4 cup ground flaxseed
- 1/4 cup sunflower seeds
- 1/4 teaspoon Kosher Salt
- Pepper to taste
- Dipping sauce of choice

INSTRUCTIONS

1. Chop peeled potato into smaller pieces. Place in a blender and pulse until the larger pieces are broken up.
2. Add in your cauliflower, onion, and garlic and pulse again.
3. Mix in the cilantro, flaxseed, sunflower seeds, arrowroot, and remaining seasonings.
4. Puree until a thick batter is formed. Place batter in a larger bowl. Scoop 1/4 cup of the batter out at a time and form into patties about 1 1/2 inches thick. Place on baking sheet. Repeat until you have about 7-10 patties.
5. Place in the freezer for about 10 minutes.
6. While waiting, heat your air fryer to 360F for 3 minutes.

7. Working in batches, place 4 cauliflower patties in the air fryer and cook for 18-20 minutes depending on the thickness of your patties. Flip patties over halfway through cooking.

NUTRITIONAL FACTS (Per Serving (1 Patty))
- ✓ 85 calories; 2.9g fat; 3g net carbs; 3g protein.

Air Fried Spring Rolls with Sweet Sour Sauce

Prep Time: 10 mins; Cook Time: 15 mins; Total Time: 25 mins.

Yield: 7 Rolls.

INGREDIENTS
- ❖ 7 spring roll wrappers
- ❖ ½ cabbage, thinly sliced
- ❖ 2 large carrots, grated on the coarse side
- ❖ a dash of say sauce
- ❖ 1 teaspoon sesame oil, optional
- ❖ egg noodles, optional
- ❖ Toasted sesame seeds
- ❖ Salt to taste
- ❖ 4-6 tablespoons olive oil
- ❖ 1 egg white, beaten
- ❖ For the Sauce
- ❖ 3/4 cup white sugar
- ❖ ¼ cup white vinegar
- ❖ A dash of soy sauce
- ❖ 2 teaspoon grated fresh ginger
- ❖ 2 full teaspoons cornflour mixed with a little water
- ❖ 2 slices of pineapple cut into very small dice

INSTRUCTIONS
1. Heat some of the oil and saute the vegetables on high heat for 1-2 minutes.
2. Add the soy, salt, and sesame oil (if using). Do not overcook. Remove from the heat and allow it to cool down and then add the toasted sesame seeds.
3. Place the spring roll wrappers on a flat surface and brush the sides with the egg white. Spoon some of the vegetable mixture onto the wrapper and fold the sides in

and then roll up. Place on a baking sheet with fold side at the bottom. Repeat until you have used up all the vegetable mix.
4. Brush the spring rolls with remaining oil and arrange in the air fryer basket. Set the air fryer to 400F and air fry for about 6 minutes.
5. Meanwhile, make the sauce by combining all the ingredients (except soy and cornflour) in a pot and boil. Add the spoil sauce and the cornflour. Serve rolls with sauce and enjoy.

NUTRITIONAL FACTS (Per Serving)
- ✓ 85 calories; 6g fat; 3g net carbs; 3g protein.

Twice Air-Fried Vegan Stuffed Potatoes with Kale

Prep Time: 10 mins; Cook Time; 20MINS; TOTAL TIMES: 30 MINS.

Yield: 4 Servings.

INGREDIENTS
- ❖ 2 red medium to large Potatoes
- ❖ 1 to 2 teaspoons olive oil, leave out to make oil-free
- ❖ 1/4 cup unsweetened vegan yogurt
- ❖ 1/4 cup unsweetened nondairy milk
- ❖ 2 tablespoons nutritional yeast
- ❖ 1/2 teaspoon kosher salt
- ❖ 1/4 teaspoon pepper
- ❖ 1 cup chopped kale
- ❖ Chopped chives

INSTRUCTIONS
1. Peel and slice the potatoes, and rub each slice with oil on all sides.
2. Preheat your air fryer to 390°F for 2-3 minutes. Add the potatoes to the air fryer basket.
3. Set the cooking time to 30 minutes and when the time is up, turn the potatoes over and cook for 30 more minutes.
4. Let the potatoes cool enough that you can touch them without burning yourself.
5. Cut each potato in half lengthwise and carefully scoop out the middle of the potato while leaving enough to create a stable shell of the potato skin and a thin layer of the white part.

6. Mash the scooped potato, vegan yogurt, milk, nutritional yeast, salt, and pepper until smooth.
7. Stir in the kale and fill the potato shells with the mixture.
8. Depending on the size of your air fryer, you may be able to cook all 4 halves at the same time or you may have to cook 2 of them at a time.
9. Cook on 390F for 5 minutes.
10. Top with chives and serve.

NUTRITIONAL FACTS (Per Serving)

- ✓ 193 calories; 7g fat; 23g net carbs; 14g protein.

Air Fried Crispy Asian Broccoli

Prep Time: 10 mins; Cook Time: 20 mins; Total Time: 30 mins

Yield: 4 servings

INGREDIENTS

- ❖ 1 pound broccoli, cut into florets
- ❖ 1 1/2 tablespoons peanut oil
- ❖ 1 teaspoon white vinegar
- ❖ 1 tablespoon minced garlic
- ❖ Fine sea salt to taste
- ❖ 2 tablespoons reduced sodium soy sauce
- ❖ 2 teaspoons agave
- ❖ 2 teaspoons Sriracha
- ❖ 1/3 cup roasted salted peanuts
- ❖ Fresh lime juice (optional)

INSTRUCTIONS

1. Toss together the broccoli, peanut oil, garlic and season with salt in a large bowl.
2. In a single layer, spread the broccoli into your air fryer basket, leaving a little space in between.
3. Cook for 20 minutes at 400F until golden brown and crispy, stirring once halfway.
4. Meanwhile, mix together the agave, soy sauce, sriracha and rice vinegar in a small, microwave-safe bowl.
5. Microwave for 15 seconds until the honey is melted.

6. Transfer the cooked broccoli to a bowl and add in the soy sauce mixture and toss to coat.
7. Add the peanuts and stir. Squeeze the lime on top (if using).
8. Serve and enjoy.

NUTRITIONAL FACTS (Per Serving)

✓ **85 calories; 7g fat; 11g net carbs; 9g protein.**

Air Fried Jalapeno Popper Stuffed Chicken Recipe

Prep Time: 10 mins; Cook Time: 12 mins; Total Time: 22 mins.
Yield: 12 Servings.

INGREDIENTS

- 12 chicken thighs, boneless and skinless
- 6 jalapenos, seeded and cut lengthwise
- 125g room temperature cream cheese
- 3 cloves garlic, minced
- 1/2 teaspoon onion powder
- 1/2 teaspoon chili powder
- 1/4 teaspoon fresh ground pepper
- 1 teaspoon salt
- 4 tablespoons avocado oil
- 1/4 teaspoon chili powder
- 1/4 teaspoon onion powder

INSTRUCTIONS

1. In a medium bowl, combine the cream cheese, garlic, onion powder, chili powder, salt, and pepper. Set aside.
2. Remove the stem of the jalapenos, cut them lengthwise, deseed.
3. Using a butter knife, add the cream cheese to each of the 12 jalapeno halves, as if you are putting butter on bread! Divide the cream cheese mixture up between all 12 halves.
4. Roll out a piece of chicken thigh so it is as flat as possible. Place a jalapeno popper on the chicken and roll it up. Use a toothpick to hold it secure.
5. Repeat the above step until all of the ingredients are used up.
6. In a small bowl, combine the avocado oil, chili, and onion powder and mix.
7. Brush the oil mixture on both sides of each piece of chicken.

8. Arrange the chicken in the air fryer basket in a single layer. Work in batches if need be.
9. Set the temperature to 380F and the timer to 12 minutes. Flip the chicken halfway through the cooking time.
10. Serve and enjoy.

NUTRITIONAL FACTS (Per Serving)

- ✓ **231 calories; 24g fat; 6g net carbs; 28g protein.**

Air Fried Chicken Wings with Honey and Sriracha Sauce

Prep Time: 10 mins; Cook Time: 35 mins; Total Time: 45 mins
Yield: 2 Servings

INGREDIENTS

- ❖ 1 pound chicken wings, tips removed and wings cut into different slices
- ❖ 1/4 cup honey
- ❖ 2 tablespoons sriracha sauce
- ❖ 1 1/2 tablespoons soy sauce
- ❖ 1 tablespoon butter
- ❖ juice of 1/2 lime
- ❖ Scallions, chopped, optional

INSTRUCTIONS

1. Set the air fryer to 360F.
2. Add the chicken wings to the air fryer basket, and air fry for 30 minutes. While air frying, turn the chicken about every 7 minutes to make sure the wings are evenly browned.
3. Meanwhile, make the sauce. Place sriracha in a saucepan, add the honey, soy, butter and lime juice. Stir and boil for 3 minutes.
4. When the chicken wings are done cooking, toss them in a bowl with the sauce until fully coated, then garnish with scallion.
5. Serve and enjoy.

NUTRITIONAL FACTS (Per Serving)

- ✓ **231 calories; 23g fat; 5g net carbs; 26g protein.**

Air Fryer Caribbean Spiced Chicken

Prep time: 10 mins; Cook Time: 10 mins; Total Time: 20 mins

Yield: 8 Servings

INGREDIENTS

- 3 pounds skinless chicken thigh fillets, bones removed.
- 1 1/2 teaspoons ground ginger
- 1 tablespoon ground coriander seed
- 1 tablespoon cayenne pepper
- 1 1/2 teaspoons ground nutmeg
- 3 tablespoons coconut oil, melted
- 1 tablespoon ground cinnamon
- Coarse ground black pepper to taste
- Salt to taste

INSTRUCTIONS

1. Place chicken on a large baking sheet with paper towels to soak up any residual liquid.
2. Salt and pepper both sides of the chicken and let the chicken sit for about 30 minutes.
3. Place coriander and cinnamon in a small bowl and mix. Add cayenne, ginger, and nutmeg, mix all to combine.
4. Coat chicken fillets with the mixture and brush both sides with coconut oil.
5. Working in batches, (depending on the size of your air fryer), place 4 chicken fillets into your air fryer basket. Do not overlap fillets.
6. Preheat air fryer to 390F for 2 minutes and cook chicken for 10 minutes.
7. Remove chicken fillets from the air fryer basket and place in an oven-safe dish, tightly covered with foil.   Keep warm in the oven, while you repeat instructions with remaining chicken fillets.
8. Serve fillets and enjoy!

NUTRITIONAL FACTS (Per Serving)

- **202 calories; 13.4g fat; 1.3g net carbs; 24.9g protein.**

Air Fryer Roasted Chickpeas Recipe

Prep Time: 5 mins; Cook Time: 21 mins; Total Time: 26 mins
Yield: 2 Servings

INGREDIENTS
- 1 can chickpeas, drained & rinsed (no sugar added)
- 1 teaspoon ground cumin
- 1 teaspoon garlic powder
- 2 teaspoons olive oil
- 1/8 teaspoon ground ginger
- 1 teaspoon ground coriander

INSTRUCTIONS
1. Place chickpeas in a medium mixing bowl and add oil, cumin, and garlic powder, stir.
2. Stir well to coat the beans in the oil and spices.
3. Add ginger and ground coriander. Mix well chickpeas are fully coated.
4. Pour the chickpeas mixture into your air fryer basket and cook on 370F for 12 minutes.
5. Stir the chickpeas and continue to cook for another 8 minutes.
6. Pull air fryer basket and stir chickpeas. Then cook for 1 minute more. This is how you continue until chickpeas are cooked to your desired texture.
7. When done air frying, serve chickpeas and enjoy.

NUTRITIONAL FACTS (Per Serving)
- ✓ 73 calories; 9g fat; 6g net carbs; 28g protein.

Air Fried Meatloaf Recipe

Prep Time: 10 mins; Cook Time: 20 mins; Total Time: 30 mins
Yield: 2 Servings

INGREDIENTS
- 1 pound lean ground beef, raw
- 1/3 cup corn flakes crumbs
- 1 teaspoon freshly ground black pepper

- ❖ 2 cloves minced garlic
- ❖ 8 ounces tomato sauce
- ❖ 1/2 medium onion, chopped
- ❖ 1 teaspoon dried basil
- ❖ 5 tablespoons reduced-sugar ketchup
- ❖ 3 teaspoons brown sugar blend
- ❖ 1 tablespoon Worcestershire sauce
- ❖ 1-2 teaspoon salt
- ❖ 1/2 tablespoon fresh Parsley, chopped

INSTRUCTIONS

1. In a shallow bowl, Place the ground beef, onion, garlic, corn flakes crumbs, salt, pepper, and 3/4 of the tomato sauce. Mix until well combined.
2. Use a paper towel to lightly coat the inside of two loaf pans with oil.
3. Split your meat mixture into two, and then place into loaf pans.
4. Make the glaze by combining the remaining tomato sauce, reduced-sugar ketchup, brown sugar, and Worcestershire sauce.
5. Brush the glaze on top and on the sides of the meatloaves.
6. Preheat air fryer to 360F.
7. Place loaves in the air fryer basket and air fry for 20 minutes. Pause after 10 minutes of air frying to re-glaze the loaves. Then continue cooking. Pause again after 17 minutes to re-glaze, and then continue cooking.
8. When done air frying, remove loaves from the air fryer, sprinkle the chopped parsley on top and allow to cool 5-10 minutes before removing from silicone pans.
9. Serve and enjoy.

NUTRITIONAL FACTS (Per Serving)

- ✓ **139 calories; 21g fat; 3g net carbs; 25g protein.**

Air Fried Sesame Ginger Carrots with Scallions

Prep Time: 10 mins; Cook Time: 7 mins; Total Time: 17 mins.

Yield: 4 servings.

INGREDIENTS

- ❖ 2 cups sliced carrots
- ❖ 1 tablespoon minced ginger

- 1 tablespoon soy sauce
- 2 tablespoons sesame oil
- 1 tablespoon chopped scallions
- 1 teaspoon sesame seeds

INSTRUCTIONS

1. Slice the carrots into a shallow bowl, add the garlic, soy sauce, and sesame oil. mix until well combined.
2. Pour the mixture into your air fryer basket.
3. Set the air fryer to 374F and cook for 7 minutes.
4. Shake the air fryer basket after 3-4 minutes and continue cooking.
5. When done cooking, transfer the carrots to a bowl and garnish with scallions and sesame seeds.
6. Serve warm and enjoy.

NUTRITIONAL FACTS (Per Serving)

- ✓ 101 calories; 2g protein; 7g net carbs; 7g fats.

Air Fried Chinese Salt and Pepper Pork Chops Recipe

Prep time: 15 mins; Cook Time: 25 mins; Total Time: 40 mins.
Yield: 2 service.

INGREDIENTS

- Pork Chops
- 1 egg white
- 1/2 teaspoon sea salt
- 1/4 teaspoon freshly ground black pepper
- 3/4 cup cornstarch
- 1 oil mister
- 2 Jalapeño Pepper stems removed, sliced
- 2 sliced Scallions
- 2 Tablespoons Canola Oil
- 1 teaspoon sea salt
- 1/4 teaspoon freshly ground black pepper

INSTRUCTIONS

1. Coat Air Fryer Basket with a thin coat of Oil. In a medium bowl, whisk together egg white, salt, and pepper until foamy.

2. Slice pork chops into cutlet pieces, leaving a little on the bones and pat dry. Add pork chop pieces to egg white mixture. Coat thoroughly. Marinate for at least 20 minutes.
3. Transfer pork chops a large bowl and add potato starch. Dredge the pork chops through the cornstarch thoroughly. Shake off pork and place into prepared Air Fryer Basket. Lightly spray pork with Oil.
4. Cook at 360 degrees for 9 minutes, shaking the basket often and spraying with oil between shakes.
5. Cook an additional 6 minutes at 400 degrees, or until the pork is brown and crispy.
6. 6   Slice Jalapeños thin and deseed. Chop scallions. Place in a bowl and set aside.
7. Heat skillet until screaming hot. Add oil, Jalapeño peppers, Scallions, salt, and pepper and cook for about a minute.
8. Add air-fried pork pieces to the skillet and toss them with the Jalapeño and Scallions. Cook pork for another minute, making sure they become coated with the hot oil and vegetables.

NUTRITIONAL FACTS (Per Serving)
✓ 351 calories; 46g net carbs; 5g protein; 14g fat.

Thai Fish Cakes with Mango Salsa

Prep time: 20 mins; Cook time: 14; Total Time: 34 mins.

Yield: 4 Servings.

INGREDIENTS
- 1 ripe mango, peeled and cut into cubes
- 1 pound white fish fillets
- 1 egg
- Juice and zest of one lemon
- 1 1/2 teaspoons red chili paste
- 3 tablespoons fresh coriander
- 1 scallion, finely chopped
- 1/2 cup ground coconut
- 1 teaspoon salt

INSTRUCTIONS

1. Place cubed mango pieces into a bowl, add 1/2 teaspoon chili paste, 1 tablespoon coriander, and the juice and zest of 1/2 lemon. Mix to combine.
2. place fish in a food processor and puree, mix in the egg, 1 teaspoon salt and the remainder of chili, lime zest and lime juice. Add the remaining coriander, 2 tablespoons coconut and chopped scallion. Mix all together to combine.
3. Place the remaining ground coconut on a plate.
4. Divide the fish mixture into 12 parts, shape each portion into round cakes and coat them with the coconut.
5. Working in batches, place half of the fish cakes into your air fryer basket and cook on 390F for 7 minutes or until they are golden brown. Repeat for the other half of the fish cakes.
6. When done, serve with mango salsa and enjoy.

NUTRITIONAL FACTS (Per Serving)

- ✓ **101 calories; 19.5g protein; 3g net carbs; 18g fats.**

Air Fryer Baked Garlic Parsley Potatoes

Prep time: 5 mins; Cook Time: 35 mins; Total Time: 40 mins

Yield: 3 Servings

INGREDIENTS

- ❖ 3 Potatoes
- ❖ 2 tablespoons Olive Oil
- ❖ 1 tablespoon salt
- ❖ 1 tablespoon Garlic
- ❖ 1 teaspoon Parsley

INSTRUCTIONS

1. Wash the potatoes and then create air holes with a fork in the potatoes.
2. Sprinkle them with the olive oil & seasonings, then coat the potatoes with the seasonings by rubbing seasonings evenly on the potatoes.
3. Place coated potatoes in the air fryer basket and cook at 392 degrees for 35 minutes or until potatoes fork tender.
4. Top with fresh parsley.

NUTRITIONAL FACTS (Per Serving)

- ✓ 213 calories; 4g fat; 35g net carbs; 4g protein.

Air Fried Cilantro Lime Shrimp Skewers

Prep Time: 5 mins; Cook Time: 10 mins; Total Time: 15 mins.

Yield: 4 Servings.

INGREDIENTS

- ❖ 1/2 pound raw shrimp, peeled and deveined
- ❖ 1/2 teaspoon garlic purée
- ❖ 1/2 teaspoon paprika
- ❖ 1/2 teaspoon ground cumin
- ❖ Juice of 1 lemon
- ❖ Salt to taste
- ❖ 1 tablespoon cilantro, chopped

INSTRUCTIONS

1. Soak 6 wooden skewers for 15-20 mins before needed.
2. Preheat air fryer to 350F.
3. Mix lemon juice, garlic, paprika, cumin and salt in a bowl. Add shrimp and stir to coat completely.
4. Thread shrimp onto the skewers.
5. Place skewers in your air fryer with little space in between.
6. Cook for 4-5 minutes, flip skewers and cook for another 5 minutes.
7. When done, transfer shrimp to a serving plate.
8. Garnish with chopped cilantro and extra lime slices and enjoy.

NUTRITIONAL FACTS (Per Serving)

- ✓ 183 calories; 12g fat; 7g net carbs; 14g protein.

Air Fryer Smoked Ribs

Prep Time: 35 mins; Cook Time: 12 mins; Total Time: 47 mins.
Yield: 6 Servings.

INGREDIENTS

- 1 slab baby back pork ribs cut into pieces
- 1/2 teaspoon smoked paprika
- 1/2 cup barbecue sauce
- Salt to taste

INSTRUCTIONS

1. Place ribs in a bowl and add the paprika and salt, mixing to coat well.
2. Then add barbecue sauce.
3. Preheat the air fryer to 350F.
4. Place ribs inside the air fryer basket (leave little space in between each rib).
5. Cook for 15 minutes or until cooked through, flipping once halfway through.

NUTRITIONAL FACTS (Per Serving)

- **147 calories; 9g protein; 9g carbs; 7g fat.**

Vegan Air Fryer Crispy Chickpea Tacos

Prep Time: 3 mins; Cook Time: 15 mins; Total Time: 18 mins.
Yield: 4 Servings.

INGREDIENTS

- 14 ounces 400g tin rinsed, and drained and dried
- 2 teaspoon olive oil
- ½ teaspoon smoked paprika
- ½ ground cumin
- Taco toppings
- Radishes thinly sliced
- Shredded cabbage
- Cranberries
- Coconut yogurt
- small corn tortillas

- ❖ Salt to taste
- ❖ Avocado
- ❖ Lime

INSTRUCTIONS

1. Preheat air fryer to 390F.
2. Mix all the ingredients together in a bowl.
3. Add the chickpeas into the air fryer basket.
4. Air fry for 15 minutes flipping halfway through.
5. Arrange tacos and top with coconut yogurt and squeeze in the lime.

NUTRITIONAL FACTS (Per Serving)

✓ 133 calories; 2g protein; 20g carbs; 3g fat.

Keto Air Fryer Hard Boiled Eggs Recipe

Prep Time: 4 mins; Cook Time: 16 mins; Total Time: 20 mins

Yield: 2 Servings

INGREDIENTS

- ❖ 4-6 eggs

INSTRUCTIONS

1. Preheat air fryer to 250F for 2 mins.
2. Place the wire rack in the air fryer basket and set the eggs on top.
3. Cook for 16 minutes.
4. Remove eggs from air fryer and place them in ice water to cool.
5. Peel and serve the eggs.

NUTRITIONAL FACTS (Per Serving)

✓ 125 calories; 11g protein; 8g fat; 0g carbs.

Gluten-free Air Fryer Steak with Herb Lemon Butter

Prep Time: 5 mins; Cook Time: 15 mins; Total Time: 20 mins

Yield: 2 Servings

INGREDIENTS

Herb Lemon Butter

- 1/2 stick unsalted butter at room temperature
- 3 tablespoons fresh parsley chopped
- 1/2 teaspoon lemon zest
- salt to taste
- 1 teaspoon thyme chopped
- Ground black pepper to taste

Steak

- 2 (8 ounces) steak
- 2 teaspoons olive oil

INSTRUCTIONS

Herb Lemon Butter

1. Place butter in a shallow bowl, add parsley, thyme. Mix together. Add lemon zest, salt, and pepper and mix well to combine.
2. Transfer mixture to parchment paper and form it into a log shape.
3. Roll the butter in the parchment to 1 1/2 inches in diameter, twisting the ends to close and refrigerate for some time.
4. Steak
5. Preheat air fryer to 400F.
6. Rub the olive oil on both sides of the steaks and season with salt and black pepper.
7. Place the steaks in your air fryer and air fry for 15 minutes or until the desired doneness, flipping halfway through cooking time.
8. When done cooking, remove steaks from the air fryer and rest for about 5 mins.
9. Place steaks on serving plate and top with refrigerated herb butter.
10. Serve and enjoy.

NUTRITIONAL FACTS (Per Serving)

- ✓ 590 calories; 45g fat; 45g protein.

Air fried Chocolate Chip Zucchini Bread

Prep Time: 10 mins; Cook Time: 20 mins; Total Time: 30 mins

Yield: 4 Servings

INGREDIENTS

- 300g zucchini, grated
- 260g brown sugar
- 3 large eggs
- 30g cocoa powder
- 1 cup Olive Oil
- 385g self-raising flour
- 200g dark chocolate chips
- 2 teaspoons Cinnamon
- Dieter's green tea
- 1 teaspoon nutmeg
- 1 tablespoon vanilla extract

INSTRUCTIONS

1. Brush the bottom, top and sides of your air fryer baking pan with some flour and set aside.
2. Crack eggs into a large mixing bowl, add olive oil, brown sugar, and vanilla extract. Mix well with a hand mixer until light and fluffy.
3. Fold in the flour, cocoa powder, and the green tea.
4. Add zucchini and dark chocolate chips.
5. Add the batter into the air fryer baking pan and set for 20 minutes on 360f.
6. Serve and enjoy.

NUTRITIONAL FACTS (Per Serving)

- ✓ **108 calories; 9g protein; 9g carbs; 6g fat.**

Air Fried Buffalo Cauliflower Wings

Prep Time: 5 mins; Cook Time: 25 mins; Total Time: 30 mins

Yield: 4 Servings

INGREDIENTS
- 1 tablespoon almond flour
- 4 tablespoons hot sauce
- 1 tablespoon avocado oil
- Salt to taste
- 1 medium head of cauliflower

INSTRUCTIONS
1. Preheat air fryer to 400F.
2. Cut cauliflower into bites washed and fully patted dry
3. In a large bowl, mix together hot sauce, almond flour, avocado oil, and salt.
4. Add the cauliflower and mix until coated.
5. Place half the cauliflower mixture into the air fryer and fry for 14 min or until the desired doneness.
6. 6. Remove the air fryer basket and shake halfway through to turn the cauliflower.
7. When done, remove and set aside.
8. Add in the second half of the cauliflower mixture and air fry for but cook it for 11 minutes.
9. Serve with some extra hot sauce for dipping.

NUTRITIONAL FACTS(Per Serving)
- 48 calories; 4g fat; 1g net carbs.

Air Fried Plantains

Prep Time: 5 mins; Cook Time: 10 mins; Total Time: 15 mins

Yield: 2 Servings

INGREDIENTS
- 1 plantain
- 3/4 teaspoon vegetable oil
- Salt to taste

INSTRUCTIONS

1. Preheat air fryer to 350F
2. Peel the plantain and cut into slices.
3. Place sliced plantain into a bowl.
4. Gently mix in the oil and salt until plantains are coated on both sides.
5. Put half the plantain slices in the air fryer basket in a single layer.
6. Air fry for 10 minutes, flipping halfway through.
7. Serve warm and enjoy.

NUTRITIONAL FACTS (Per Serving)

- ✓ 123 calories; 1g protein; 2g fat; 26g net carbs.

Air Fried Tater Tots Recipe

Prep Time: 15 mins; Cook Time: 20 mins; Total Time: 35 mins

Yield: 4 Servings

INGREDIENTS

- ❖ 6 large potatoes
- ❖ 1 teaspoon garlic powder
- ❖ 2 tablespoons cornflour
- ❖ 1 1/2 teaspoons dried oregano
- ❖ Salt to taste

INSTRUCTIONS

1. Preheat the air fryer to 350F.
2. Peel and rinse the potatoes.
3. Boil the potatoes till they are half cooked and then plunge them into cold water to cool them.
4. Shred the potatoes into a large bowl, then squeeze out any excess water.
5. Mix in the garlic powder, cornflour, oregano, and salt. Then form the mixture into individual tater tots.
6. Place half of the tater tots into the air fryer basket leaving little space in between.
7. Cook for 8 minutes, then flip the tater tots and continue cooking for another 7 minutes, flip then cook for a further 5 minutes until evenly browned.
8. Remove the tater tots from the air fryer and keep warm. Repeat instructions for the remaining batch of tater tots.

9. Serve with tomato sauce for dipping and enjoy.

NUTRITIONAL FACTS (Per Serving)
✓ 204 calories; 8g protein; 44g carbs; 8g fiber.

Air Fried Rosemary Turkey Breast with Maple Mustard Glaze

Prep Time: 10 mins; Cook Time: 30 mins
Total Time: 40 mins

INGREDIENTS
- 2 1/2 pounds turkey breast loin
- 1/4 cup maple syrup
- 1/4 cup Olive Oil
- 2 cloves garlic, minced
- 2 teaspoons
- 2 teaspoon chopped fresh rosemary
- 1 tablespoon butter
- 1 tablespoon ground brown mustard
- 1 teaspoon crushed pepper

INSTRUCTIONS
1. In a small bowl, mix together olive oil, garlic, chopped rosemary, salt, and pepper.
2. Spread the oil-herb seasoning evenly on both sides of the turkey breast loins. Cover and refrigerate for about 2 hours.
3. Take out turkey breast loins from the fridge at least half an hour before cooking.
4. Grease your air fryer basket and place turkey breast loins on it.
5. Cook for on 400F for 20 minutes.
6. While cooking loins, melt a tablespoon of butter in a microwave-safe bowl.
7. Add maple syrup and brown mustard and mix well to combine.
8. Liberally spread the maple-mustard glaze on the cooked turkey breast loins.
9. Return the fryer basket to the fryer and cook on 400F for another 10 minutes.
11. Let it rest for 5 to 10 minutes before slicing.
12. Serve warm with your choice of side dish.

NUTRITIONAL FACTS (Per Serving)

- ✓ 412 calories; 70g protein; 9g carbs; 9g fat.

Air Fried Lemon Green Beans

Prep Time: 10 mins; Cook Time: 12 mins; Total Time: 22 mins

Yield: 4 Servings

INGREDIENTS

- ❖ 2 cups green beans.
- ❖ 1/4 teaspoon oil
- ❖ Juice from 1 lemon
- ❖ Salt to taste
- ❖ Ground black pepper to taste

INSTRUCTIONS

1. Wash green beans and remove stems
2. Place beans in your air fryer.
3. Add lemon juice.
4. Add salt and pepper.
5. Drizzle oil over top.
6. Air fry on 400 degrees for 12 minutes.
7. Serve and enjoy.

NUTRITIONAL FACTS (Per Serving)

- ✓ 36 calories; 4g net carbs; 2g protein.

Air Fried Mini Nutella Apple Pies

Prep Time: 35 mins; Cook Time: 30 mins; Total: 1 hour 5 mins.

Yield: 6 Pies.

INGREDIENTS

Crust

- 1 1/2 cups flour
- 1/4 teaspoon salt
- 1 teaspoon organic sugar
- 1 stick unsalted butter, cold, diced into pieces
- 5 tablespoons ice water

Filling

- 1/4 cup Nutella
- 1 egg, beaten
- 4 apples, peeled, cored, and chopped
- Juice and zest from 1 lemon
- 2 1/2 tablespoons organic sugar
- 2 tablespoons flour
- 1/4 teaspoon nutmeg
- 1 teaspoon cinnamon
- 1/4 teaspoon salt
- More butter
- Cinnamon and sugar-spice mix, divided

INSTRUCTIONS

1. Place the flour, salt, and sugar in a bowl and mix well to combine.
2. Then, using your hands, add the butter into pea-sized pieces form.
3. Drizzle in 4 tablespoons of ice water and mix until the dough comes together. If necessary, add the last tablespoon of ice.
4. Form dough into a flat disk, wrap in plastic wrap and refrigerate for 30 minutes.
5. Meanwhile, make the filling. Place all the filling ingredients (except for the cinnamon and sugar-spice mix) in a bowl. Stir together until well combined. Set aside until ready.
6. Sprinkle flour on a flat surface and roll out the pie dough until it's about 1/2 inch thick.
7. Press the ramekin in the dough lightly and using a pairing knife, cut out 12 circles (of dough).

8. Place one circle of dough into the bottom of each ramekin and press up the sides of the dish.
9. Divide the mixture between the six ramekins.
10. Top the mixture with a few small dots of butter. Top with the other dough circles and seal the sides.
11. Using a paring knife, gently cut 3 slits in the top, brush with an egg wash, and sprinkle
12. with the cinnamon and sugar-spice mix. Place in your air fryer basket and air fry on 350F for 30 minutes or until tops are crispy and golden brown.
13. Devour!

NUTRITIONAL FACTS (Per Serving)

✓ **264 calories; 33g net carbs; 12.8g fat; 3g protein.**

Air Fried Tomato and Onion Quiche

**Prep Time: 10 mins; Cook Time: 30 mins; Total: 40 mins.
Yield: 1 Serving.**

INGREDIENTS
- 2 eggs
- 1/2 cup shredded cheese
- 1/4 cup milk
- 1/4 cup diced tomatoes
- 2 tablespoons diced onion
- Salt to taste

INSTRUCTIONS

1. Crack the eggs into a ramekin, add the cheese, tomatoes, onion, and salt. Mix together until well combined.
2. Place ramekin in your air fryer basket and air 340F for 30 minutes.
3. Serve and enjoy.

NUTRITIONAL FACTS (Per Serving)

✓ **264 calories; 3g net carbs; 12.8g fat; 13g protein.**

Air Fryer Cauliflower Tater Tots

Prep Time: 25 mins; Cook Time: 10 mins; Total Time: 35 mins

Yield: 6 Servings

INGREDIENTS

- 1 head of cauliflower, chopped
- 2 eggs
- 1/4 cup all-purpose flour
- 1/2 cup Parmesan cheese, grated
- 1 teaspoon salt
- freshly ground black pepper to taste
- Oil in a spray bottle

INSTRUCTIONS

1. Place the chopped cauliflower in the center of a clean kitchen towel and twist the towel tightly to drain water from the cauliflower.
2. Place the cauliflower in a large bowl. Add the eggs, flour, Parmesan cheese, salt and freshly ground black pepper.
3. Shape the cauliflower into small tater tot shapes, rolling one tablespoon of the mixture at a time.
4. Place the tots on a cookie sheet lined with paper towel to absorb any residual moisture.
5. Spray cauliflower tots all over with oil.
6. Place cauliflower in your air fryer basket and air fry on 400F for 10 minutes, flipping them over for the last few minutes of the cooking process.
7. Season with salt and black pepper.
8. Serve hot with your favorite sauce for dipping.
9. ENJOY!

NUTRITIONAL FACTS (Per Serving)

- **109 calories; 13g net carb; 6g fat; 2g protein.**

Air Fried Rice with Sesame and Sriracha Sauce

Prep Time: 10 mins; Cook Time: 20 mins; Total Time: 30 mins.
Yield: 2 Servings.

INGREDIENTS

- 1 teaspoon sriracha
- 2 cups cooked white rice
- 1 tablespoon vegetable oil
- 2 teaspoons toasted sesame oil
- Kosher salt to taste
- 1 tablespoon water
- Freshly ground black pepper to taste
- 1 teaspoon soy sauce
- 1/2 teaspoon toasted sesame seeds, plus extra for topping
- 1 large egg, lightly beaten
- 1 cup frozen peas and carrots, thawed

INSTRUCTIONS

1. Place the rice in a shallow bowl, add vegetable oil, 1 teaspoon of the sesame oil, 1 tablespoon water, salt, and pepper. Toss to coat the rice, and then transfer to a foil pan that fits into your air fryer.
2. Put the pan in your air fryer and air fry on 350F for 12 minutes until the rice is lightly toasted and crunchy, make sure to stir halfway through.
3. Meanwhile, make the sauce by combining the sriracha and soy sauce in another small bowl. Add sesame seeds and the remaining 1 teaspoon sesame oil. Mix well to combine and set aside.
4. Open the air fryer and pour the egg over the rice. Close and cook for about 4-5 minutes or until the egg is cooked through.
5. Open again, stir in the peas and carrots, then close and continue to cook for an additional 2 minutes.
6. When done cooking, spoon the fried rice into two bowls, drizzle with some of the sauce and garnish with more sesame seeds.
7. Serve and enjoy.

NUTRITIONAL FACTS (Per Serving)

- **264 calories; 27g net carbs; 9g fat; 7g protein.**

Air Fryer Mini Swedish Meatballs

Prep Time: 10 mins; Cook Time: 15 mins; Total Time: 25 mins.

Yield: 42 mini meatballs.

INGREDIENTS

- ounces ground beef
- 2 slices white bread
- 1/2 cup milk
- 1 large egg
- 8 ounces ground pork
- 1/4 yellow onion, grated
- 3/4 teaspoon ground allspice
- 1 teaspoon fine sea salt
- Freshly ground black pepper to taste
- Lingonberry jam

INSTRUCTIONS

1. Put the milk in a medium bowl. Place the bread in the bowl with the milk and let soak for 5 minutes.
2. Remove bread after 5 mins and squeeze out excess milk. Tear it into bite-size pieces.
3. Crack the egg into a shallow bowl, mix in the ground beef, pork, onion, and allspice. Add the bread pieces and mix well to combine, then season with 1 teaspoon salt and pepper to taste and stir. Form mixture into small balls about the size of a heaping tablespoon.
4. Spray the basket of your air fryer with cooking spray and fill it with the meatballs.
5. Set your air fryer to 360F and air fry for about 10 minutes shaking the basket halfway through, until browned, tender and cooked through.
6. When done cooking, serve with lingonberry jam and enjoy.

NUTRITIONAL FACTS (Per Serving)

- ✓ 264 calories; 5g net carbs; 11g fat; 12g protein.

Air Fried Banana Bread

Prep Time: 15 mins; Cook Time: 30 mins; Total Time: 45 mins.

Yield: 4 Servings.

INGREDIENTS
- 2 ripe bananas
- 1/2 cup all-purpose flour
- 1/4 cup vegetable oil
- 1/4 cup whole wheat flour
- 1/2 teaspoon kosher salt
- 1/4 teaspoon baking soda
- 1/2 cup granulated sugar
- 1/4 cup plain yogurt
- 1/2 teaspoon pure vanilla extract
- 1 large egg

INSTRUCTIONS
1. Prepare a medium bowl, place the flour in it and mix in the wheat, salt, and baking soda.
2. Place the bananas in another medium bowl and mash them until very smooth in.
3. Add the sugar, oil, yogurt, vanilla, and egg to the banana and stir until smooth.
4. Sift the dry ingredients over the wet and fold together with a spatula until just combined.
5. Scrape the batter into a metal pan that can fit into your air fryer and smooth the top.
6. Put the pan in your air fryer, set air fryer on 310F and air fry for 30 minutes or until a toothpick inserted in the middle of the bread comes out clean. Be sure to turn the pan halfway while cooking.
7. Transfer the pan to a rack to cool for 5-10 minutes. Unmold the banana bread from the pan and let cool completely on the rack.
8. Once cooled, slice the banana bread into wedges, serve and enjoy.

NUTRITIONAL FACTS (Per Serving)
- **230 calories; 9g fat; 32g carbs; 1g fiber; 5g protein.**

Air Fried Lamb Rack with Macadamia Rosemary Crust

Prep Time: 10 mins; Cook Time: 30 mins; Total Time: 40 mins

Yield: 4 Servings

INGREDIENTS

- 1 3/4 pounds lamb rack
- 2 1/2 ounces macadamia nuts, chopped
- 1 large egg
- 1 tablespoon breadcrumbs (I used panko)
- 1 tablespoon olive oil
- 1 tablespoon fresh rosemary, chopped
- I clove chopped garlic
- Kosher salt to taste
- Ground black pepper to taste

INSTRUCTIONS

1. In a small bowl, combine the olive oil and the chopped garlic.
2. Brush the lamb rack with the oil mixture and generously season with salt and pepper.
3. Place chopped macadamia in a bowl, add the breadcrumbs and rosemary, stir to combine.
4. Crack the egg into a separate bowl and mix well.
5. Dip the lamb first into the egg and ensure it is well coated, take out and drain off excess. Then dip the lamb rack into the nut mixture to coat.
6. Place the lamb rack in your air fryer basket and air fry on 350F for 25 minutes.
7. Flip the lamb rack and increase the heat to 400F and then continue to cook for another round of 10 minutes.
8. When done cooking, remove meat from air fryer and, allow it to cool for 5-10 minutes, covered in aluminum foil.
9. After cooling, slice and serve.

NUTRITIONAL FACTS(Per Serving)

- **435 calories; 36g fat; 1g net carbs; 26g protein.**

Air Fryer Roasted Paprika Potatoes with Greek Yoghurt

Prep Time:10 mins; Cook Time: 20 mins; Total Time: 30 mins.

Yield: 4 Servings.

INGREDIENTS

- 1 3/4 pounds waxy potatoes, peeled
- 2 tablespoons olive oil
- 1/2 cup Greek yogurt
- 1 teaspoon spicy paprika
- Pepper to taste
- Salt to taste

INSTRUCTIONS

1. Slice the potatoes and cut each slice into small cubes.
2. Soak potatoes cubes in water for 30 minutes or more, then remove from water, drain, and pat dry with paper towel.
3. Place 1/2 of the olive oil in a medium bowl and mix in paprika and pepper. Evenly coat the potatoes in the mixture and transfer the coated potato cubes into your air fryer.
4. Set the air fryer to 356F and air fry potato cubes for 2o minutes or until brown, flipping 2-3 times while cooking.
5. Meanwhile, place the Greek yogurt in a small bowl, mix in the remaining oil, salt, and pepper.
6. Place the potato cubes on a serving plate, sprinkle with paprika and garnish with the yogurt as a dip.
7. ENJOY!

NUTRITIONAL FACTS(Per Serving)

- ✓ **435 calories; 9g fat; 19g net carbs; 24g protein .**

Air Fryer Stuffed Portobello Mushrooms

Prep Time: 20 mins; Cook Time: 20 mins; Total Time: 40 mins.

Yield: 2 Servings.

INGREDIENTS

- 1/4 cup breadcrumbs
- 1/4 cup grated Pecorino-Romano
- 2 tablespoons shredded mozzarella
- 1 tablespoon chopped fresh parsley
- 1 teaspoon chopped fresh mint
- 1 clove garlic, minced
- 1 1/2 pounds Portobello mushrooms, stems removed
- 4 tablespoons olive oil
- Kosher salt to taste
- Ground black pepper to taste

INSTRUCTIONS

1. Get a medium shallow bowl and put the bread crumbs in it. Mix in the next five ingredients. Add 2 tablespoons oil, salt and pepper, and mix.
2. Toss the mushrooms with the remaining 2 tablespoons olive oil in a large bowl and arrange on a small baking sheet with the cavities facing up.
3. Divide the breadcrumb mixture among the mushrooms, filling the cavities and pressing down gently to secure.
4. Place half the mushrooms in a single layer in your air fryer basket and air fry om 360F for 10 minutes or until the filling is bubbling and browned.
5. Repeat instructions with the remaining batch of portobello mushrooms.
6. Serve when done and enjoy.

NUTRITIONAL FACTS (Per Serving)

- 85 calories; 9g fat; 14g net carbs; 21g protein.

Air Fryer Cheese Loaf Recipe

Prep Time: 37 mins; Cook Time: 18 mins; Total Time: 55 mins

Yield: 4 Servings

INGREDIENTS

- 1/2 cup whole wheat flour
- 1/2 cup plain flour
- 7g instant yeast
- 1/2 cup grated cheese, plus more for sprinkling
- 1/2 cup lukewarm water
- 2/3 teaspoon kosher salt

INSTRUCTIONS

1. Combine the wheat flour and plain flour in a bowl with salt and mix. Add the yeast and cheese, stir to combine. While stirring, add 1 cup lukewarm water and mix until the dough forms a softball.
2. Knead the dough for about 5 minutes until it becomes smooth and elastic. Then shape it into a ball and place in a bowl. Cover the bowl with a lid and allow it to rise in a warm place for about 30 minutes.
3. Preheat your air fryer to 400°F. Brush the top of the dough with water and sprinkle more cheese on top.
4. Place dough in a small cake pan (must fit into your air fryer) and put the pan in the fryer basket and slide the basket into the air fryer. Turn the timer to 18 minutes and bake the bread until it is golden brown and cooked through. Allow the bread to cool on a wire rack and Serve.

NUTRITIONAL FACTS (Per Servings)

- **86 calories; 18g fat; 9g net carbs; 17g protein.**

Air Fried Fish and Chips Recipe

Prep Time: 15 mins; Cook Time: 15 mins; Total Time: 30 mins.

Yield: 2 Servings.

INGREDIENTS

- 200 g white fish fillets
- 1 egg
- 30 g finely ground tortilla chips
- 300 g potatoes
- 1 tablespoon olive oil
- 1/2 tablespoon lemon juice

INSTRUCTIONS

1. Scrub the potatoes clean and cut them lengthwise into thin strips, then soak in water for 30 minutes. Drain and pat dry with a paper towel. Coat them with oil in a boil.
2. Meanwhile, cut the fish into four equal parts and rub with lemon juice, salt, and pepper. Let the fish sit for 5 minutes.
3. Place ground tortilla chips on a plate.
4. Crack the egg in a dish and stir to combine.
5. Dip each piece of fish part first into the egg and then roll through the tortilla chips so that they are evenly covered.
6. Insert the separator in the air fryer basket. Position the potato strips on one side and the pieces of fish on the other and air fry on 356F for 12-15 minutes or until they are crispy brown.
7. Serve and enjoy.

NUTRITIONAL FACTS (Per Servings)

- **110 calories; 18g fat; 6g net carbs; 17g protein.**

Air Fryer Fried Pickles with Italian Seasoning

Prep Time: 20 mins; Cook Time: 10 mins; Total Time: 30 mins.

Yield: 6 Servings.

INGREDIENTS
For the Pickles
- One 16-ounce jar dill pickle chips
- 1 1/2 cups breadcrumbs
- 1/2 cup all-purpose flour
- 1 cup buttermilk
- 1/4 teaspoon ground cayenne pepper
- 1 1/2 teaspoons Cajun seasoning
- 1 teaspoon hot sauce
- 1 teaspoon Italian seasoning
- 1/2 teaspoon kosher salt
- 1 tablespoon olive oil

For the Sauce
- 1/2 cup mayonnaise
- 1 teaspoon prepared horseradish
- 4 teaspoons ketchup
- 1/2 teaspoon Cajun seasoning

INSTRUCTIONS
For the pickles
1. Preheat your air fryer to 390F.
2. Set a wire rack inside a baking sheet.
3. Drain the pickles and spread them out on a paper towel-lined baking sheet. Pat dry with more paper towels. Eliminate any pickles with large holes or ones that are very thin.
4. Place the flour, cayenne and 1/2 teaspoon Cajun seasoning in one bowl.
5. In another bowl, mix the buttermilk and hot sauce.
6. In yet a separate bowl, combine the breadcrumbs, Italian seasoning, the remaining 1 teaspoon Cajun seasoning and 1/2 teaspoon salt. Drizzle in the oil and use your hands to toss and coat the breadcrumbs.
7. Working in small batches, first, toss a handful of pickles in the flour mixture, shaking off any excess.

8. Then duck them in the buttermilk mixture to completely coat, shaking to remove any excess. Also, toss them in the breadcrumbs.
9. Arrange the breaded pickles on the prepared baking sheet and repeat until all the pickles are breaded.
10. Arrange one-third of the breaded pickles in the basket of your air fryer in a single layer.
11. Cook for 8-10 minutes, or until pickles are crunchy and browned on both sides.
12. 12. Remove from the air fryer and transfer to a serving plate.   Repeat with the remaining batches of pickles.
13. For the sauce
14. In a bowl, whisk together the mayonnaise, horseradish, ketchup, and Cajun seasoning.
15. Serve the warm pickles with the sauce for dipping.

NUTRITIONAL FACTS (Per Servings)
- ✓ 86 calories; 9g fat; 9g net carbs; 11g protein.

Air Fryer Roast Chicken with Rosemary

Prep Time: 10 mins; Cook Time: 55 mins; Total Time: 65 mins.

Yield: 3 servings.

INGREDIENTS
- ❖ 3 pounds chicken
- ❖ 1 tablespoon olive oil
- ❖ 1/2 lemon
- ❖ 3 sprigs fresh rosemary
- ❖ Sage
- ❖ 4 cloves garlic, minced
- ❖ Kosher salt to taste
- ❖ Freshly ground black pepper, taste

INSTRUCTIONS
1. Preheat your air fryer to 370F and spray the basket with nonstick cooking spray.
2. Rub the outside of the chicken with the olive oil.
3. Sprinkle the chicken inside and outside with 1 tablespoon salt and several grinds of pepper. Fill the cavity with the herbs, garlic, and lemon. Put the chicken in the basket breast-side up.

4. Air fry the chicken on 165F for 55 minutes or until it is golden and crispy.

NUTRITIONAL FACTS (Per Serving)

- ✓ **290 calories; 1.4g carbs; 17.2g fat; 30.8g protein.**

Air Fried Spicy Drumsticks with Barbecue Marinade

Prep Time: 10 mins; Marinate Time: 20 mins; Cook Time: 30 mins; Total Time: 1 hr.

Yield: 4 Servings.

INGREDIENTS

- ❖ 1 clove garlic, crushed
- ❖ 2 teaspoons brown sugar
- ❖ 4 drumsticks
- ❖ Freshly ground black pepper
- ❖ ½ tablespoon mustard
- ❖ 1 teaspoon chili powder
- ❖ 1 tablespoon olive oil

INSTRUCTIONS

1. Mix the garlic with the mustard, brown sugar, chili powder, a pinch of salt and freshly ground pepper to taste. Mix with the oil.
2. Rub the drumsticks completely with the marinade and leave to marinate for 20 minutes.
3. Put the drumsticks in the basket and air fry at 392°F to 10 minutes until brown.
4. Then reduce the temperature to 300°F and cook for another 10 minutes until done.
5. Serve the drumsticks with corn salad and enjoy.

NUTRITIONAL FACTS (Per Serving)

98 calories; 1.4g carbs; 17.2g fat; 19.8g protein.

Air Fried Bread Recipe

Prep Time: 1 hr 10 mins; Cook Time: 20 mins; Total Time: 1 hr 30 mins.

Yield: 1 loaf of bread.

INGREDIENTS

- 2 2/3 cups all-purpose flour
- 3 tablespoons + 2 teaspoons unsalted butter, melted
- 1 1/2 teaspoons active dry yeast
- 1 1/2 teaspoons sugar
- 1 1/2 teaspoons kosher salt

INSTRUCTIONS

1. Grease a pan that can fit into your air fryer with 2 teaspoons butter and set aside.
2. Combine the 3 tablespoons butter, yeast, sugar, salt and 1 cup warm water in a stand mixer fitted with the dough hook attachment. With the mixer on low speed, add 1/2 cup of the flour at a time.
3. Once all of the flour is added, knead on medium speed for 8 minutes.
4. Transfer the dough to the prepared pan, cover and let rise until doubled in size, about 1 hour.
5. Place the pan with the dough in your air fryer and set to 380F and air fry for 20 minutes or until the bread is dark brown and the internal temperature registers 200F.
6. Take off the air fryer and let it cool in the pan for 5 minutes, then turn out onto a rack to cool completely.
7. Enjoy with your favorite sauce.

NUTRITIONAL FACTS (Per Serving)

- **115 calories; 9g net carbs; 6g fat; 3g protein**

Air Fried Prawns with Cocktail Sauce

Prep Time: 10 mins; Cook Time: 6 mins;Total Time:16 mins

Yield: 4 servings for four people

INGREDIENTS

For the Prawn

- fresh king prawns
- 1 teaspoon chili flakes
- 1 teaspoon chili powder
- 1/2 teaspoon fine sea salt
- 1/2 teaspoon freshly ground black pepper or to taste

For the Sauce

- 3 tablespoons mayonnaise
- 1 tablespoon wine vinegar
- 1 tablespoon ketchup

INSTRUCTIONS

1. Place the chili powder in a bowl, add the flakes, salt, and pepper and mix well.
2. Add the prawns and toss to coat them in the spice mixture.
3. Place the spicy prawns into your air fryer basket and air fry on 356°F for about 8 minutes.
4. While prawns are cooking, prepare the sauce. Mix the sauce ingredients in a bowl.
5. Serve the hot prawns with the cocktail sauce and enjoy.

NUTRITIONAL FACTS(Per Serving)

- **170 calories; 13g fat; 1g carbs; 12g protein.**

Air Fried Ricotta Balls with Chives

Prep Time: 15 mins; Cook Time: 16 mins; Total Time: 31 mins.

Yield: 20 balls.

INGREDIENTS

- 1 cup ricotta
- 1 tablespoon chives
- 1 teaspoon olive oil
- 3 slices stale white bread
- 2 tablespoons flour
- 1 head basil, chopped
- 1 egg, yolk separated from the white
- 1 teaspoon salt, or more to taste
- Pepper to taste

INSTRUCTIONS

1. Place the ricotta in a bowl with the flour and mix.
2. Add the egg yolk, 1 teaspoon salt, and freshly ground pepper and mix to combine.
3. Stir in the chives and basil.
4. Divide the mixture into 20 equal portions and shape them into balls. Let the balls rest for a while.
5. Using a food processor, grind the bread slices into fine bread crumbs and mix with the olive oil. Pour the mixture into a deep dish.
6. Beat the egg white in another deep dish.
7. Evenly coat the ricotta balls in the egg white and then in the bread crumbs.
8. Divide the balls into two equal batches and cook each batch in your air fryer at 392°F for 8 minutes or until golden brown.
9. Transfer ricotta balls to a serving plate and enjoy.

NUTRITIONAL FACTS (Per Serving)

- **290 calories; 1.4g carbs; 17.2g fat; 30.8g protein.**

Air Fried Puff Pastry Bites Recipe

Prep Time: 10 mins; Cook Time: 20 mins; Total Time: 30 mins.

Yield: 9 portions.

INGREDIENTS

- 200 g ready-made puff pastry, frozen
- 2 tablespoons milk
- 1/2 large apple
- 1 tablespoon fresh mint, chopped
- 1 tablespoon finely chopped preserved ginger

INSTRUCTIONS

1. Start by chopping the apple into small pieces, place into a bowl. Add the fresh mint and chopped ginger.
2. Cut the pastry into 16 squares of the desired size.
3. Scoop a heaped teaspoon of apple mixture onto each square.
4. Fold the squares into triangles and moisten the edges with some water and press the edges firmly together with a fork.
5. Put eight squares into your air fryer basket and brush them with milk. Slide the basket into the air fryer cook at 392°F for 10 minutes until they are golden brown.
6. Repeat instructions for the remaining 8 squares.
7. Serve and enjoy.

NUTRITIONAL FACTS (Per Serving)

- ✓ **85 calories; 7g fat; 11g net carbs; 9g protein**

Air Fried Basil-Parmesan Salmon Recipe

Prep time; 5 mins; Cook Time: 16 mins; Total Time: 21 mins.

Yield: 4 Servings.

INGREDIENTS

- 4 salmon fillets, skin removed (20 ounces)
- 1/2 lemon
- 1/4 teaspoon Kosher salt
- 3 tablespoons mayonnaise
- 6 fresh basil leaves, minced (plus more for garnish)
- 3 tablespoons Parmesan cheese, grated
- Ground black pepper to taste

INSTRUCTIONS

1. Season each salmon fillet with lemon juice, salt, and pepper.
2. Place the mayonnaise in a small bowl, add basil and 2 tablespoons parmesan cheese and mix well to combine.
3. Evenly spread the parmesan mixture over the top of each fillet.
4. Sprinkle the remaining parmesan cheese on top.
5. Spray your air fryer basket with olive oil.
6. Working in batches, cook each batch at 400F for 8 minutes.
7. Serve garnished with fresh basil and enjoy.

NUTRITIONAL FACTS (Per Serving)

- **289 calories; 30g protein; 1g carbs; 19g protein.**

Air Fried Chicken Chimichanga Recipe

Prep Time: 15 mins; Cook Time: 20 mins; Total Time: 35 mins.

Yield: 4 Servings.

INGREDIENTS

For the Pico de Gallo

- 1/2 cup diced tomato
- 3 tablespoons chopped onion
- 2 tablespoon chopped fresh cilantro

- ❖ 1 teaspoon fresh lime juice
- ❖ 1/4 teaspoon kosher salt
- ❖ Freshly ground black pepper

For The Chimichangas
- ❖ ounces shredded leftover chicken breast
- ❖ Juice of 1/2 navel orange
- ❖ Juice of 1/2 lime
- ❖ 1 large garlic clove, minced
- ❖ 1 teaspoon ground cumin
- ❖ 1 can (4 ounces) mild diced green chiles, drained
- ❖ 4 whole-wheat tortillas
- ❖ 1/2 cup shredded pepper Jack cheese
- ❖ 3 cups shredded lettuce
- ❖ 4 tablespoons sour cream
- ❖ 1/2 small avocado, diced
- ❖ Olive oil spray

INSTRUCTIONS

Make the pico de gallo

1. Combine the tomato, lime juice, and onion in a small bowl. Add 1 tablespoon cilantro, salt, and pepper to taste. Mix to blend and set aside.
2. Make the chimichanga
3. Combine the chicken and orange juice in a large bowl. Add the lime juice, cumin, chiles, and garlic. Mix together until well combined.
4. On a work surface, working with one at a time, place 3/4 cup of the chicken mixture onto the bottom third of a tortilla. Sprinkle each with 2 tablespoons cheese. Lift the edge nearest you and wrap it around the filling. Fold the left and right sides in toward the center and continue to roll into a tight cylinder. Set aside, seam side down, and repeat with the remaining tortillas and filling.
5. Lightly spray all sides of the chimichangas with oil. Place 2 of the chimichangas seam side down in the air fryer basket and air fry on 400°F for 8 minutes, flipping halfway, until golden and crispy. Repeat instructions with the remaining chimichangas.
6. To serve
7. Place 3/4 cup shredded lettuce on each plate. Place a chimichanga on top, along with 2 tablespoons pico de gallo, 1 tablespoon sour cream, and 1-ounce avocado and garnish with 1 tablespoon cilantro. Serve and enjoy.

NUTRITIONAL FACTS (Per Serving)

- ✓ 391 calories; 40g protein; 12g net carbs; 18.5g fat.

Air Fried Apricot and Blackberry Crumble Recipe

Prep Time: 10 mins; Cook Time: 20 mins; Total Time: 30 mins.

Yield: 4 Servings.

INGREDIENTS

- ❖ 2/3 cup fresh blackberries
- ❖ 250 g fresh apricots
- ❖ 3 1/2 tablespoons cold butter, in cubes
- ❖ 6 tablespoons sugar
- ❖ 1 tablespoon lemon juice
- ❖ 1 tablespoon water
- ❖ 100 g flour
- ❖ Pinch of salt

INSTRUCTIONS

1. Halve the apricots and remove the stones. Cut the apricots into cubes and mix them in a bowl with the lemon juice and 2 tablespoons sugar.
2. Grease a cake tin that can fit into your air fryer basket and spread the fruit mix over the tin.
3. Place the flour in a bowl with a pinch of salt. Add the remaining sugar, the butter, and 1 tablespoon water and make it into a crumbly mixture using your fingertips.
4. Evenly spread the crumbly mixture over the fruit and press the top layer lightly.
5. Put the cake tin in the basket and slide the basket into the air fryer. Set your air fryer to 400F and air fry 20 minutes until golden brown and done.
6. Serve the crumble whipped cream if desired.

NUTRITIONAL FACTS (Per Serving)

- ✓ 115 calories; 9g net carbs; 6g fat; 3g protein.

Air Fryer Mushroom CroQuettes Recipe

Prep Time: 15 mins; Cook Time: 10 mins; Total Time: 25 mins.

Yield: 8 portions.

INGREDIENTS

- 100 g chopped mushrooms
- 1 small onion, chopped
- 1 1/4 tablespoon butter
- 1½ heaped tablespoons flour
- 50 g breadcrumbs
- 2 cups milk
- Kosher salt to taste
- Ground nutmeg, to taste
- 2 tablespoons vegetable oil

INSTRUCTIONS

1. Melt the butter in a saucepan and fry the onion and mushrooms.
2. Add the flour and stir.
3. Warm up the milk and add it little by little, to the saucepan.
4. Keep stirring until the mixture thickens, then season with salt and nutmeg. Leave to cool then refrigerate for 2 hours.
5. Meanwhile, mix the oil and breadcrumbs together and stir continuously until the mixture becomes loose and crumbly again.
6. Roll 1 tablespoon of mushroom mixture in the breadcrumbs until it is completely coated. Repeat instructions until all the mushroom mixture is used up.
7. Preheat your air fryer to 400° F.
8. Place the mushroom croquettes in your air fryer basket air fry for 8 minutes until they are browned and crispy.

NUTRITIONAL FACTS(Per Serving)

- **105 calories; 9g net carbs; 6g fat; 3g protein.**

Air Fried Potato Croquettes with Parmesan Cheese Recipe

Prep Time: 30 mins; Cook Time: 10 mins; Total Time: 40 mins.

Yield: 4 Servings.

INGREDIENTS

- 300 g starchy potatoes, peeled and cubed
- 1/2 cup shredded Parmesan cheese
- 1 egg yolk
- 2 tablespoons flour
- Freshly ground pepper to taste
- Ground nutmeg to taste
- 50g bread crumbs

INSTRUCTIONS

1. Boil the potato cubes in salted water for 15 minutes until ready. Drain the potatoes and mash them finely with a potato masher. Allow the mashed potatoes to cool.
2. Add the egg yolk, cheese, flour, and chives to the potato puree and mix well. Then season with salt, pepper, and nutmeg.
3. Preheat the air fryer to 400°F.
4. Mix the oil and the bread crumbs and keep stirring until the mixture becomes loose and crumbly again.
5. Shape the potato puree into 12 croquettes and roll them through the bread crumbs until they are evenly coated.
6. Put six croquettes in the fryer and air fry for 4 minutes until they are crispy and browned. Repeat instructions with the remaining croquettes.
7. Serve and enjoy.

NUTRITIONAL FACTS (Per Serving)

- 254 calories; 21g net carbs; 6g fat; 3g protein.

Air Fried Asian-Glazed Boneless Chicken Thighs Recipe

Prep Time: 5 mins; Cook Time: 30 mins; Marinate Time: 2 hrs; Total Time: 2 hrs 35 mins.

Yield: 8 Servings.

INGREDIENTS

- 32 ounces 8 boneless, skinless chicken thighs, fat trimmed
- 1/4 cup low sodium soy sauce
- 2 1/2 tablespoons balsamic vinegar
- 1 tablespoon honey
- 3 cloves crushed garlic
- 1 teaspoon Sriracha hot sauce
- 1 teaspoon fresh grated ginger
- 1 scallion, sliced

INSTRUCTIONS

1. Combine the balsamic, soy sauce, honey, garlic, sriracha and ginger in a small bowl. Mix well until combined.
2. Pour 1/4 cup of the marinade into a large bowl with the chicken, covering all the meat and marinate for 2 hours.
3. Remove the chicken from the marinade and transfer to your air fryer basket.
4. Cook in batches at 400F for 14 minutes, turning halfway until cooked through in the center.
5. Meanwhile, place the remaining sauce in a small pot and cook over medium-low heat for 2 minutes or until it reduces slightly and thickens.
6. When done, spread the sauce over the chicken and garnish with sliced scallions.

NUTRITIONAL FACTS (Per Serving)

✓ **297 calories; 45g protein; 4g net carbs; 9.5g fat.**

Air fried Stuffed Bagel Recipe

Prep Time: 5 mins; Cook Time: 30 mins; Total Time: 35 mins.

Yield; 4 Servings.

INGREDIENTS
- 1 cup unbleached all-purpose flour
- 2 teaspoons baking powder
- 3/4 teaspoon kosher salt
- 1 cup non-fat Greek yogurt
- 1 egg, beaten
- Dried garlic flakes
- Onion flakes, dried.

INSTRUCTIONS
1. Combine the flour, baking powder and salt in a bowl and whisk well.
2. Add the yogurt and mix with a spatula until well combined to look like small crumbles.
3. Lightly dust flour on a work surface and remove dough from the bowl, knead the dough 15-20 times until dough is tacky, but not sticky.
4. Divide into 4 equal balls. Roll each ball into 3/4-inch thick ropes and join the ends to form bagels.
5. Whisk the egg into a small bowl.
6. Top with egg and sprinkle both sides with garlic and onion flakes.
7. Preheat the air fryer 280F. Working in batches, transfer into the air fryer and air fry for 15 minutes, or until golden.   Let cool at for 10-15 minutes before cutting.
8. Serve.

NUTRITIONAL FACTS (Per Serving)
- ✓ 152 calories; 24g net carbs; 10g protein.

Air Fried Parmesan Garlic Knots with Parsley

Prep Time: 10 mins; Cook Time: 25 mins; Total Time: 35 mins.

Yield: 8 Servings.

INGREDIENTS
- 1 cup all-purpose flour
- 3/4 teaspoon kosher salt
- 2 teaspoons baking powder
- 1 cup fat-free Greek Yogurt, drained of any excess liquid
- 2 teaspoons butter
- 3 cloves garlic, chopped
- 1 tablespoon grated parmesan cheese
- 1 tablespoon finely chopped fresh parsley
- Olive oil spray

INSTRUCTIONS
1. Combine the flour, baking powder and salt in a large bowl and whisk well. Add the yogurt and mix until well combined. Then use your dry hands and knead about 15 times. Add more water if it's too sticky. Roll into a dough.
2. Divide the dough into 8 equal pieces then roll each piece into worm-like strips of 9 inches long.
3. Tie each breadstick into a "knot-like" ball; divide into batches.
4. Preheat your air fryer to 325F.
5. Place the first batch into the air fryer basket. Spray with olive oil and air fry 11 minutes until golden.
6. Repeat with the remaining batch. Let them cool for 5 minutes.
7. Meanwhile, melt butter in a medium nonstick skillet, add the garlic and cook until golden, 2 minutes.
8. Use a brush to cover the knots with the garlic.
9. Sprinkle with parmesan cheese and chopped parsley.

NUTRITIONAL FACTS (Per Serving)
- **87 calories; 5g protein; 12g net carbs; 2g fat.**

Air Fried Buffalo Chicken Egg Rolls Recipe

Prep Time: 15 mins; Cook Time: 30 mins; Total Time: 45 mins.

Yield: 8 Servings.

INGREDIENTS

- 2 boneless skinless chicken breasts, (8 ounces each), cooked
- 2 ounces cream cheese, softened
- 1/2 cup hot sauce
- 1/2 cup crumbled blue cheese
- 1/3 cup shredded carrots, chopped
- 1/3 cup chopped scallions
- 16 egg roll wrappers
- olive oil spray
- Blue Cheese Dressing, optional

INSTRUCTIONS

1. Shred cooked chicken with forks into a bowl and set aside.
2. In a large bowl, combine the cream cheese and hot sauce together until smooth. Add the shredded chicken, blue cheese, carrots and scallions, and mix until well combined.
3. One at a time, place egg roll wrapper on a clean surface, points facing top and bottom like a diamond.
4. Spoon out 3 tablespoons of the buffalo dip mixture onto the bottom third of the wrapper.
5. Dip your finger in a small bowl of water and run it along the edges of the wrapper. Lift the point nearest you and wrap it around the filling.
6. Fold the left and right corners inward to the center and continue to roll into a tight cylinder.
7. Set aside and repeat with remaining wrappers and filling.
8. Spray all sides of the egg rolls with oil.
9. Working in batches, cook at 370F for 9 minutes, flipping halfway through until golden brown.
10. Serve warm with sauce for dipping, if you desire.

NUTRITIONAL FACTS (Per Serving)

- **231 calories; 6g fat; 24g carbs; 1g fiber; 20g protein.**

Air Fried Cauliflower Rice Balls Recipe

Prep Time: 5 mins; Cook Time: 25 mins; Total Time: 30 mins.

Yield: 2 Servings.

INGREDIENTS

- 1 Italian chicken sausage link, casing removed
- 2 1/4 cups riced cauliflower
- 1/4 teaspoon kosher salt, more to taste
- 3 tablespoons marinara
- 1/2 cup part-skim shredded mozzarella
- 1 large egg, beaten
- 1/4 cup bread crumbs
- 1 tablespoon grated parmesan
- Cooking spray

INSTRUCTIONS

1. Cook the sausage for 5 minutes in a medium skillet over medium-high heat, breaking it up with a spoon as small as you can.
2. Add the cauliflower, salt, and marinara and cook 6 minutes on medium heat, stirring until the cauliflower is tender and heated through.
3. Remove from heat and add the mozzarella cheese to the skillet and stir well to mix. Let it cool 3 minutes until you can easily handle it.
4. Spray a 1/4 measuring cup with cooking spray and fill it to the brim with cauliflower mixture. Use a small spoon to scoop out into your palm and roll into a ball. Set aside on a dish.
5. Repeat with the remaining cauliflower, to make 6 balls.
6. Place the egg in one bowl and the breadcrumbs in another.
7. Add the parmesan to the crumbs and mix.
8. Dip the ball in the egg, then in the crumbs and transfer to your air fryer. Spray with cooking spray and air fry at 400F for 9 minutes turning halfway until golden.
9. When done cooking, serve warm with 1 tablespoon marinara sauce.

NUTRITIONAL FACTS (Per Serving (Makes 3 Rice Balls))

- **257 calories; 11g net carbs; 22g protein; 12g fat.**

Air Fried Mascarpone Mushroom Pasta Recipe

Prep Time: 10 mins; Cook Time: 15 mins; Total Time: 35 mins.

Yield: 4 bowls.

INGREDIENTS

- 4 cups sliced mushrooms
- 1/2 cup shredded parmesan cheese
- 2 teaspoons minced garlic
- 1/4 cup cream
- ounces mascarpone cheese diced
- 1 teaspoon dried thyme
- 1 teaspoon ground black pepper
- 1/2 teaspoon red pepper flakes
- 1 cup chopped onion
- 1 teaspoon salt

INSTRUCTIONS

1. Grease a pan that can fit into your air fryer and set aside.
2. Combine the mushrooms, garlic, cream, cheese, onion, thyme, salt, pepper, and red pepper flakes. Mix and pour into greased pan and place in your air fryer
3. Set air fryer to 350°F and air fry for 15 minutes, stirring mixture halfway through.
4. Meanwhile, boil 4 cups of pasta until al dente. Then divide across four bowls.
5. Remove the mushrooms and mascarpone mixture from the air fryer and divide evenly on the pasta.
6. Sprinkle the Parmesan cheese on top, serve and enjoy.

NUTRITIONAL FACTS (Per Serving)

- ✓ **402 calories; 12g protein; 9g net carbs; 35g fat.**

Air Fried Cilantro Pesto Chicken Legs with Lemon

Prep Time: 10 mins; Cook Time: 20 mins; Total Time: 30 mins.

Yield: 2 Servings.

INGREDIENTS

- 1/2 cup cilantro
- 4 chicken drumsticks
- 1/2 Jalapeño pepper
- cloves Garlic
- 2 thin slices ginger
- 2 tablespoons lemon juice
- 2 tablespoons oil
- 1 teaspoon fine sea salt

INSTRUCTIONS

1. Chop all the vegetables: cilantro, pepper, garlic, and ginger, and place in a small bowl. Add salt, oil and lemon juice and mix well.
2. Rub the mixture evenly on the chicken drumsticks and marinate in the refrigerator for at least 30 minutes.
3. When you are ready to cook, place the chicken legs into your air fryer basket, skin side up.
4. Set your air fryer to 390F for 20 minutes or until doneness, flipping halfway through.
5. Remove chicken from air fryer and serve.

NUTRITIONAL FACTS (Per Serving)

- **412 calories; 5g net carbs; 34g fat; 22g protein.**

Air Fried Spicy Lamb Sirloin Steak Recipe

Prep Time: 10 mins; Marinate Time: 30 mins; Cook Time: 15 mins; Total Time: 55 mins.

Yield: 4 Servings.

INGREDIENTS

- 1 pound boneless lamb sirloin steaks
- 4 slices ginger
- 5 cloves garlic
- 1/2 onion
- 1 teaspoon ground cinnamon
- 1 teaspoon garam masala
- 1 teaspoon ground fennel
- 1/2 teaspoon ground cardamom
- 1 teaspoon cayenne
- 1 teaspoon salt

INSTRUCTIONS

1. Combine all the ingredients except the lamb steaks into a blender bowl.
2. Pulse until all ingredients are finely blended.
3. Place the lamb steaks into a large bowl and use a knife to slice into the meat and fat.
4. Add the blended spice paste and mix well.
5. Refrigerate the mixture for at least 30 minutes.
6. Set your air fryer to 330F. Place the lamb steaks in a single layer in the air fryer basket and air fry for 15 minutes or until an instant-read thermometer inserted reads an internal temperature of 150F. Flip lamb steaks halfway while cooking.
7. Serve with your favorite side dish and enjoy.

NUTRITIONAL FACTS (Per Serving)

- **182 calories; 24g protein; 2g net carbs; 7g fat.**

Keto Air Fried Lasagna Recipe

Prep Time: 15 mins; Cook Time: 30 mins; Total Time: 45 mins.

Yield: 4 Servings.

INGREDIENTS

- 1 zucchini, thinly sliced
- 1 cup prepared marinara sauce

For the Meat

- 1/2 pound Italian sausage
- 1 cup white onion, diced
- 1 teaspoon minced garlic

For the Cheese

- 1/2 cup shredded mozzarella cheese
- 1/2 cup shredded parmesan, divided
- 1/2 cup ricotta cheese
- 1 egg
- 1/2 teaspoon garlic minced
- 1/2 teaspoon Italian Seasoning
- 1/2 teaspoon ground black pepper

INSTRUCTIONS

1. Spray a pan that can fit into your air fryer with oil and arrange the zucchini in overlapping layers in the bottom of the pan. Spread 1/4 cup of marinara sauce on top of the zucchini.
2. Mix the onions, garlic, and Italian sausage together in a large bowl. Layer the meat on top of the zucchini and spread the mixture evenly. Evenly spread the rest of the marinara sauce.
3. Place the ricotta in a bowl and mix in mozzarella and 1/4 of a cup of the parmesan cheese. Spread the cheese mixture on top of the meat.
4. Top with the remaining 1/4 cup parmesan cheese. Cover the pan with foil.
5. Set your air fryer to 350F and air fry for 20 minutes. Then, remove the foil and fry for another 10 minutes until the top is browned and bubbling. Remove the lasagna and let it rest for 10 minutes before you unfasten from the pan. Serve and enjoy.

NUTRITIONAL FACTS (Per Serving)

- **350 calories; 27g fat; 6g net carbs; 17g protein.**

Air Fried Taco Meatballs Recipe

Prep Time: 1o mins; Cook Time: 15 mins; Total Time: 25 mins.

Yield: 4 Servings.

INGREDIENTS

- 1 pound lean hamburger
- 1/4 cup finely minced onions
- 1/4 cup cilantro chopped
- 1 tablespoon minced garlic
- 2 tablespoons taco seasoning
- 1 egg
- Kosher salt to taste
- Ground black pepper to taste
- 1/2 cup Mexican Blend Shredded Cheese

For Dipping Sauce

- 1/4 cup sour cream
- 1-2 teaspoons Cholula hot sauce
- 1/2 cup salsa

INSTRUCTIONS

1. In a stand mixer bowl, combine the hamburger, onions, cilantro, garlic, and egg. Add salt, pepper an add the shredded cheese.
2. Beat the mixture together with the paddle attachment for 2 minutes or until it forms a sticky paste.
3. Form the mixture into 12 meatballs.
4. Place meatballs in the air fryer basket. Set the air fryer to 400F and air fry meatballs for 10 minutes.
5. While cooking meatballs, Place the sour cream in a small bowl, mix in the salsa, and hot sauce.
6. Serve with the meatballs.

NUTRITIONAL FACTS (Per Serving)

- ✓ **320 calories; 18g fat; 5g carbs; 33g protein.**

Air Fried Chicken Jalfrezi Recipe

Prep Time: 10 mins; Cook time: 15 mins; Total Time; 25 mins.

Yield: 4 Servings.

INGREDIENTS

- 1 pound Boneless Skinless Chicken Thighs cut into large, 2 inch pieces
- 1 cup Onion, diced
- 2 cups chopped bell pepper
- 2 tablespoons oil
- 1 teaspoon Garam Masala
- 1/2 teaspoon cayenne
- 1 teaspoon Turmeric
- 1 teaspoon salt

For the Sauce

- 1/4 cup tomato sauce
- 1 tablespoon water
- 1 teaspoon Garam Masala
- 1/2 teaspoon cayenne
- 1/2 teaspoon salt

INSTRUCTIONS

1. Place chicken in a large bowl, add the onions, peppers, oil, salt, turmeric, garam masala, and cayenne. Mix together to combine.
2. Preheat your air fryer to 360F.
3. Place the chicken mixture in the air fryer basket and
4. air fry for 15 minutes. Stir and toss chicken mixture halfway through.
5. Meanwhile, in a small microwave-safe bowl, combine tomato sauce, water, garam masala, salt, and cayenne.
6. Microwave for 1 minute. Remove and stir. Microwave for another minute. Then set aside.
7. Once the chicken mixture is cooked to doneness, remove from the air fryer and place it in a large bowl.
8. Pour the prepared sauce over them, and toss to cover the chicken and vegetables completely with the sauce. Serve and enjoy.

NUTRITIONAL FACTS (Per Serving)

- **247 calories; 23g protein; 6g net carbs; 12g protein.**

Keto Air Fried Salmon Vegetables Recipe

Prep Time: 20 mins; Cook Time: 15 mins; Total Time: 35 mins.

Yield: 2 Servings.

INGREDIENTS

- 2 salmon fillets (5 ounces each)
- 1 tablespoon olive oil
- 2 garlic cloves minced
- 1 tablespoon fresh ginger, minced
- 1/2 cup fresh orange juice
- 1/4 cup Soy Sauce
- 3 tablespoons Rice Vinegar
- 2 teaspoons finely grated orange zest
- 1/2 teaspoon salt
- 2 ounces shiitake mushrooms (stems removed)
- 2 heads baby bok choy halved length-wise
- 1/2 teaspoon toasted Sesame Seeds
- 1 tablespoon Dark Sesame Oil
- Kosher salt to taste

INSTRUCTIONS

1. Whisk the garlic and ginger together in a small bowl. Add the orange zest and juice, soy sauce, vinegar, olive oil, and salt and mix well.
2. Place salmon in a gallon-size resealable bag. Pour half of the ginger mixture over the salmon fillets. Seal the bag and shake to coat. Allow it to marinate at room temperature for about 30 minutes.
3. Meanwhile, brush the mushroom caps and bok choy all over with sesame oil and season with salt.
4. After marinating, place salmon fillets in your air fryer basket and air fry on 400°F for 12 minutes or until doneness.
5. Add the vegetable mixture halfway through cook time.
6. When done, remove salmon vegetables from the air fryer and drizzle with some of the reserved marinade.
7. Sprinkle with sesame seeds. Serve and enjoy.

NUTRITIONAL FACTS (Per Serving)

- ✓ 190 calories; 4g protein; 10g net carbs; 14g fat.

Air Fried Korean Chicken Wings with Gochujang & Mayonnaise Dressing

Prep Time: 10 mins; Cook Time: 30 mins; Total Time: 40 mins.
Yield: 4 Servings.

INGREDIENTS

For the Wings
- 2 pounds chicken wings
- 1 teaspoon fine sea salt
- 1 teaspoon ground black pepper

For the Dressing
- 1 tablespoon mayonnaise
- 2 tablespoons gochujang
- 1 tablespoon Sesame Oil
- 1 tablespoon minced ginger
- 1 teaspoon agave nectar
- 1 tablespoon garlic, minced
- 2 packets sugar
- 2 teaspoons Sesame Seeds optional
- 1/4 cup onions, chopped (optional)

INSTRUCTIONS

1. Preheat your air fryer to 400°F for 2 minutes
2. Generously season the chicken wings with salt and pepper and place in the air fryer basket and air fry for 20 minutes or until a meat thermometer reads 160F, Flip chicken wings once halfway through.
3. Meanwhile, prepare the dressing. Mix all the dressing ingredients together and let the mixture marinate for a few minutes until chicken finish cooking.
4. When done air frying chicken wings, remove them from the air fryer and place into a bowl. Pour about half the dressing on the wings, and toss to coat completely.
5. Place the chicken wings back into the air fryer and air fry 5 minutes more until the dressing has glazed over, and the chicken has reached 165F.
6. Remove chicken finally from the air fryer, sprinkle with sesame seeds green onions and serve.

NUTRITIONAL FACTS (Per Serving)
- ✓ 350 calories; 23g protein; 5g carbs; 26g fat.

Air Fried Scotch Eggs with Pepper Sauce Recipe

Prep Time: 20 mins; Cook Time: 15 mins; Total Time: 35 mins.

Yield: 4 Servings.

INGREDIENTS
- ❖ 4 hard-boiled eggs, peeled
- ❖ 1 pound pork sausage
- ❖ 2 tablespoons chopped fresh parsley
- ❖ 1/8 teaspoon nutmeg, grated
- ❖ 1 tablespoon fresh chives, chopped
- ❖ 1/8 teaspoon kosher salt
- ❖ 1/8 teaspoon black pepper
- ❖ 1 cup shredded Parmesan cheese
- ❖ 2 teaspoons ground mustard
- ❖ Nonstick vegetable oil spray

INSTRUCTIONS
1. Combine the sausage, mustard, chives, and parmesan in a large bowl and blend. Mix in parsley, nutmeg, salt, and pepper. Mix until is well combined, then shape the mixture into four patties of equal sizes
2. Please each egg on a sausage patty and roll sausage around egg. Dip each in parmesan cheese to completely cover, pressing lightly to adhere.
3. Arrange the eggs in your air fryer basket. Spray lightly with nonstick vegetable oil and air fry on 400°F for 15 minutes. Halfway through cook time, flip eggs over eggs and spray with vegetable oil.
4. Serve with mustard and enjoy.

NUTRITIONAL FACTS (Per Serving)
- ✓ 530 calories; 43g fats; 1g net carbs; 32g protein.

Air Fried Chicken with Indian Fennel Recipe

Prep Time: 10 mins; Cook Time: 15 mins; Total Time: 25 mins.

Yield: 4 Servings.

INGREDIENTS

- 1 pound boneless skinless chicken thighs each thigh cut into 3 pieces
- 1 teaspoon ground fennel seeds
- 1 large onion, sliced thick
- 1 tablespoon coconut oil
- 2 teaspoons minced garlic
- 1 teaspoon smoked paprika
- 1 teaspoon garam masala
- 2 teaspoons minced ginger
- 1 teaspoon turmeric
- 1 teaspoon salt
- 1 teaspoon cayenne
- 2 teaspoons fresh lemon juice
- 1/4 cup Chopped parsley
- Vegetable Oil spray

INSTRUCTIONS

1. Mix all the ingredients together in a bowl and allow the chicken to marinate for at least 30 minutes.
2. Place chicken and vegetables into the air fryer basket. Spray the chicken and onion with some vegetable oil.
3. Cook on 360F for 15 minutes. Spray the chicken with more vegetable oil halfway through, and shake it.
4. When done air frying, remove the chicken and vegetables from the air fryer and transfer to a serving plate.
5. Sprinkle with fresh lemon juice and parsley.
6. Serve and enjoy.

NUTRITIONAL FACTS (Per Serving)

- **190 calories; 4g carbs; 8g fat and 22g protein.**

Air Fried Pork Chops with Vietnamese Thit Nuong

Prep Time: 40 mins; Cook Time: 10 mins; Total Time: 50 mins.

Yield: 4 Servings.

INGREDIENTS

- 1 pound pork shoulder
- 1/4 cup minced onions
- 2 tablespoons oil
- 2 tablespoons sugar
- 2 teaspoons dark soy sauce
- 1 tablespoon Fish Sauce
- 1 tablespoon minced lemongrass paste
- 1 tablespoon garlic, minced
- 1/2 teaspoon Ground Black Pepper
- 2 tablespoons chopped cilantro
- 1/4 cup roasted peanuts, crushed

INSTRUCTIONS

1. Prepare a bowl. Combine the onions, sugar, soy sauce, and oil together. Add the garlic, fish sauce, lemongrass, and pepper. Mix all to combine.
2. Slice the pork shoulder thin into 1/2 in slices, and then cut crossways into 4-inch pieces.
3. Add the pork to the onion mixture and marinate for 30 minutes.
4. Remove the pork slices from the marinade, and place in single layer in the air fryer basket.
5. Set the air fryer to 400°F and cook the pork for 10 minutes, flipping over halfway through.
6. Use a meat thermometer to test the pork and ensure it has reached an internal temperature of 165°.
7. Remove from the air fryer and transfer it to a serving plate.
8. Sprinkle with the roasted peanuts and garnish with cilantro and enjoy.

NUTRITIONAL FACTS (Per Serving)

- **230 calories; 16g protein; 3g net carbs; 16g fat.**

Air Fried Brazilian Tempero Baino Chicken Drumsticks

Prep Time: 5 mins; Cook Time: 25 mins; Total Time: 30 mins.

Yield: 4 Servings.

INGREDIENTS

- 1 1/2 pounds chicken drumsticks
- 1 teaspoon cumin seeds
- 2 tablespoons oil
- 1 teaspoon dried Oregano
- 1 teaspoon turmeric
- 1 teaspoon salt
- 1/2 teaspoon coriander seeds
- 1/2 teaspoon whole black peppercorns
- 1 teaspoon dried Parsley
- 1/2 teaspoon Cayenne
- 1/4 cup lime juice

INSTRUCTIONS

1. Combine the cumin, oregano, parsley, salt, coriander seeds, peppercorns, turmeric, and cayenne pepper together in a grinder and blend.
2. Place the ground spices in a medium bowl, and the lime juice and oil and combine. Add the chicken drumsticks and turn them, coating well with the marinade. Refrigerate the chicken for at least 30 minutes.
3. Place the chicken skin side up into your air fryer basket and air fry on 390F for 25 minutes, turning the chicken legs halfway through.
4. When done cooking, remove chicken from air fryer and serve.

NUTRITIONAL FACTS (Per Serving)

- 186 calories; 14g protein; 2g net carbs; 14g fat.

Air Fried Cornish Game Hens Recipe

Prep Time: 45 mins; Cook Time: 20 mins; Total Time: 65 mins.

Yield: 4 Servings.

INGREDIENTS

- 2 whole cornish game hens giblets removed, split in half length-wise
- 1/4 cup Fish Sauce
- garlic cloves peeled and smashed
- 1 Jalapeño pepper chopped
- 1 tablespoon soy sauce
- 2 teaspoon Ground Black Pepper
- 2 teaspoon ground coriander
- 2 tablespoon lemongrass paste
- 2 tablespoon stevia
- Kosher salt
- 1 cup fresh cilantro leaves and stems trimmed and chopped coarsely
- 1 teaspoon turmeric

INSTRUCTIONS

1. Place the four halves of the Cornish game hens into a large bowl.
2. In a blender jar, add the cilantro, fish sauce, garlic, sugar, lemongrass paste, pepper, coriander, salt and turmeric, and process until smooth. Pour the mixture over the chicken and mix very well and, then refrigerate for at least 30 minutes.
3. Place the game hen halves in a single layer in your air fryer basket and cook on 400F for 20 minutes. Chicken should reach an internal temperature of 150ºF.
4. Remove chicken from the air fryer and transfer to a platter and enjoy.

NUTRITIONAL FACTS (Per Serving)

- ✓ **186 calories; 16g protein; 2g net carbs; 15g fat.**

Air Fried Mini Quiche Wedges with Mushroom

Prep Time: 10 mins; Cook Time: 15 mins; Total Time: 35 mins.

Yield: 9 Servings.

INGREDIENTS

- 100 g chilled ready-made pie crust dough
- 1/2 tablespoon oil
- 1 egg
- 3 tablespoons whipping cream
- 40 g grated cheese
- Freshly ground pepper
- 2 small pie moulds of 10 cm
- 125 g mushrooms, sliced
- 1 clove garlic, minced
- 1 teaspoon of paprika
- 1 tablespoon olive oil

INSTRUCTIONS

1. Heat a pan greased with olive oil. Add the mushroom and paprika and cook on high 2-3 or until browned. Set aside.
2. Cut two rounds of 15 cm from the dough. Lightly grease the moulds with oil and line them with the dough. Press the dough down along the edges.
3. 8   Lightly beat the egg with the cream and the cheese and season with salt and pepper to taste. Pour the mixture into the moulds and divide the mushroom mixture between the moulds.
4. Place mold in your air fryer basket and set the air fryer 400°F and air fry for 12 minutes until golden brown and ready. Repeat procedures for the other quiche.
5. Remove the quiches from the moulds and cut each quiche into 6 wedges.
6. Serve the quiche wedges and enjoy.

NUTRITIONAL FACTS (Per Serving)

- **142 calories; 3g net carbs; 11g protein; 10g fat.**

Air Fried Brown Nut Loaf Recipe

Prep Time: 37 mins; Cook Time: 18 mins; Total Time: 55 mins.

Yield: 4 Servings.

INGREDIENTS

- 1 cup plain flour
- 7g instant yeast
- 1/2 chopped hazelnuts
- 2/3 teaspoon kosher salt
- 1/2 cup lukewarm water

INSTRUCTIONS

1. In a mixing bowl, combine the plain flour with salt and mix. Add the yeast and chopped hazelnuts and stir. While stirring, add water and mix until the dough forms a soft ball.
2. Knead the dough until it becomes smooth and elastic. Then shape it into a ball and place in a bowl covered with a plastic wrap. Place in a warm place for about 30 minutes to rise.
3. Preheat your air fryer to 400°F.
4. Brush the top of the bread with water. Place it in a small cake pan that fits into your air fryer and put the pan in the fryer basket. Turn the timer to 18 minutes and air fry the dough until golden brown and doneness.
5. Allow the bread to cool on a wire rack and serve to enjoy.

NUTRITIONAL FACTS (Per Serving)

- 185 calories; 3g carbs; 18g fat; 9g protein.

Air Fried Beef Rib Croquettes

Prep Time: 15 mins; Cook Time: 5 mins; Total Time: 30 mins.

Yield: 8 Servings.

INGREDIENTS

- 100 g beef rib, finely chopped
- 1 small onion, chopped
- 1 1/4 tablespoon butter
- 1½ heaped tablespoons flour

- ❖ 50g breadcrumbs (I used panko)
- ❖ 2 cups milk
- ❖ Sea salt to taste
- ❖ Ground nutmeg, to taste
- ❖ 2 tablespoons vegetable oil

INSTRUCTIONS

1. Melt the butter in a saucepan and fry the onion and beef rib. Add the flour and stir.
2. Warm up the milk and add it little by little, to the saucepan. Keep stirring until the mixture thickens, then season with salt and nutmeg. Leave to cool then refrigerate for 1-2 hours.
3. Meanwhile, mix the oil and breadcrumbs together and stir continuously until the mixture becomes loose and crumbly again.
4. Roll 1 tablespoon of beef mixture in the breadcrumbs until it is completely coated. Repeat instructions until all the beef mixture is used up.
5. Preheat your air fryer to 400°F for 2 minutes.
6. Place the beef croquettes in your air fryer basket air fry for 8 minutes until they are browned and crispy.

NUTRITIONAL FACTS (Per Serving)

✓ **83 calories; 5g carbs; 5g protein; 4g fat.**

Air Fried Salmon Spring Onion CroQuettes with Garlic

Prep Time: 10 mins; Cook Time: 10 mins; Total Time: 20 mins.

Yield: 2 Servings.

INGREDIENTS

- ❖ 1 tin salmon (180g), drained and flaked
- ❖ 4 tablespoons sliced spring onion
- ❖ 1 egg
- ❖ 4 tablespoons finely chopped celery
- ❖ 1/2 teaspoon garlic granules
- ❖ 5 tablespoons wheat germ
- ❖ 1 tablespoon chopped fresh dill
- ❖ Non-skillet vegetable oil spray

INSTRUCTIONS

1. Combine the salmon, celery, and green onion in a medium bowl, Mix in the egg, dill, and garlic.
2. Shape the mixture into golf ball-like shape, and roll in wheat germ to coat. Flatten the balls slightly, spray with vegetable oil and place in your air fryer basket.
3. Cook in the air fryer at 400F for about 10 minutes, flipping over as needed, until golden brown.
4. Transfer to a serving dish and enjoy.

NUTRITIONAL FACTS (Per Serving)

- ✓ 85 calories; 5g carbs; 10g protein; 8g fat.

Air Fried Roasted Chicken with Buttermilk Marinade

Prep Time: 5 mins; Marinate Time: 30 mins; Cook Time: 50 mins; Total Time: 1 hr 25 mins. Yield: 4 Servings.

INGREDIENTS

- ❖ 3 pounds whole chicken, trimmed
- ❖ 2 cups low-fat buttermilk
- ❖ 3 teaspoons Kosher or more salt to taste

INSTRUCTIONS

1. Put the whole chicken into a large resealable bag or container and season it with 2 teaspoons salt. Pour the buttermilk into the bag or container and shake to coat. Seal the bag and place it in the fridge to marinate anywhere from 30 minutes.
2. Remove chicken from the fridge at least 60 minutes before cooking. Shake chicken to remove excess milk, and then discard the buttermilk.
3. Preheat your air fryer to 350F 2-3 minutes.
4. Place the chicken belly side down in the air fryer basket and season chicken top with 1/2 teaspoon salt.
5. Cook in the air fryer for 25 minutes, flip over and season with remaining salt, then continue to cook 25 more minutes or until crispy and browned on all sides.
6. Remove chicken from air fryer and transfer to a platter and let it rest for 5-10 minutes before slicing.
7. Slice chicken and enjoy.

NUTRITIONAL FACTS (Per Serving)

- ✓ 186 calories; 4g carbs; 14g fat; 16g protein.

Air Fied Twice Fried Plantains

Prep Time: 5 mins; Cook Time: 20 mins; Total Time: 30 mins.

Yield: 2 Servings.

INGREDIENTS

- ❖ 1 large green plantain, peeled
- ❖ 1 cup of water
- ❖ 1 teaspoon kosher salt
- ❖ olive oil spray
- ❖ 3/4 teaspoon garlic powder

INSTRUCTIONS

1. After peeling the plantain, cut it into 1-inch pieces to give 8 pieces in total.
2. Combine the water with salt and garlic powder in a small bowl.
3. Preheat the air fryer to 400F for 3 minutes.
4. Spray the plantain with olive oil and cook 6 minutes. Repeat instructions with remaining pieces if working in batches.
5. Remove from the air fryer and while they are hot mash them with the bottom of a jar to flatten.
6. Dip them in the water mixture and set aside.
7. Preheat the air fryer to 400F once again and cook, in batches 5 minutes on each side, spraying both sides of the plantains with olive oil.
8. When done, spray with more oil and season with salt.
9. ENJOY!

NUTRITIONAL FACTS (Per Serving)

- ✓ 124 calories; 25g cabs; 2g fat; 3g protein.

Air Fried Ham-King Prawns with Red Pepper Dip and Paprika

Prep Time: 15 mins; Cook Time: 13 mins; Total Time: 28 mins.

Yield: 10 Servings.

INGREDIENTS

- 5 slices of raw ham
- 1 large red bell pepper, halved
- 1 tablespoon olive oil
- frozen king prawns, defrosted
- 1 large clove garlic, crushed
- ½ tablespoon paprika
- Freshly ground black pepper

INSTRUCTIONS

1. Put the bell pepper in the basket and slide it into the air fryer. Set the air fryer to 425F and air fry the bell peppers for 10 minutes.
2. Put the bell pepper in a bowl and cover it. Let it rest for 15 minutes.
3. Peel the prawns, make an incision in the back and remove the black vein. Halve the slices of ham lengthwise and wrap each prawn in a slice of ham.
4. Coat the parcels with a thin film of olive oil and put them in the basket. Slide the basket into the air fryer and air fry for 3 minutes until crispy.
5. In the meantime, peel the skin of the bell pepper halves, remove the seeds and cut the pepper into pieces. Puree the bell pepper in the blender with the garlic, paprika and olive oil. Pour the sauce into a dish and season with salt and pepper to taste.
6. Serve the prawns in ham in a platter with tapas forks and add the small dish with red pepper dip.

NUTRITIONAL FACTS (Per Serving)

- 191 calories; 6g cabs; 9g fat; 11g protein.

Air Fried Cinnamon Rolled Meat

Prep Time: 15 mins; Cook Time: 40 mins; Total Time: 55 mins.

Yield: 4 Servings.

INGREDIENTS

- 1 teaspoon cinnamon
- 1 500g turkey breast fillet (you can use pork)
- 1 clove garlic, crushed
- 1½ teaspoon ground cumin
- 2 tablespoons olive oil
- 1 small red onion, finely chopped
- 1/2 teaspoon chili powder
- 3 tablespoons flat-leafed parsley, finely chopped
- String for rolled meat

INSTRUCTIONS

1. Place the meat on a cutting board with the short side towards you and slit horizontally along the full length about a 1/3 of the way from the top stopping 2 cm from the edge. Fold this part open and slit it again from this side and open it.
2. In a large bowl, combine the garlic in a bowl with the chili powder, cinnamon, cumin, pepper, and 1 teaspoon salt. Mix in the olive oil. Spoon 1 tablespoon of this mixture in another small bowl. Mix the onion and parsley in the mixture in the large bowl.
3. Preheat the air fryer to 356°F.
4. Coat the meat with the onion mixture. Roll the meat firmly, start at the short side. Tie the string around the meat at 3 cm intervals. Rub the outside of the rolled meat with the herb mixture.
5. Place the meat in the air fryer basket and air fry for 40 minutes or until doneness.

NUTRITIONAL FACTS (Per Serving)

✓ **191 calories; 5g cabs; 9g fat; 19g protein.**

Air Fried Lamb Loin Chops with Za'atar

Prep Time: 5 mins; Cook Time: 10 mins; Total Time: 15 mins.

Yield: 4 servings.

INGREDIENTS

- bone-in lamb loin chops, trimmed (3 ½ ounces each)
- 3 cloves garlic, crushed
- 1 teaspoon extra-virgin olive oil
- 1/2 fresh lemon
- 1 1/4 teaspoon kosher salt
- 1 tablespoon Za'atar
- Fresh ground pepper, to taste

INSTRUCTIONS

1. Rub the lamb chops with oil and garlic.
2. Squeeze the lemon over both sides, then season with salt, zatar and black pepper.
3. Preheat the air fryer to 400F. In batches in an even layer, cook to desired liking, about 10 minutes flipping halfway through.
4. Serve and enjoy.

NUTRITIONAL FACTS (Per Serving)

- 424 calories; 5g carbs; 34g fat; 22g protein.

Air Fried Turkish Chicken Recipe

Prep Time: 45 mins; Cook Time: 15 mins; Total Time: 60 mins.

Yield: 4 Servings.

INGREDIENTS

- 1 pound skinless chicken thighs, bones removed
- 1 tablespoon garlic, minced
- 1 tablespoon tomato paste
- 1 tablespoon vegetable Oil
- 1 tablespoon lemon juice
- 1 teaspoon ground cumin
- 1 teaspoon smoked paprika
- 1/2 teaspoon ground cinnamon

- 1/4 cup plain Greek yogurt
- 1/2 teaspoon ground black Pepper
- 1 teaspoon fine sea salt
- 1/2 teaspoon cayenne

INSTRUCTIONS

1. Combine the Greek yogurt, garlic, tomato paste, lemon juice, oil, and salt together in a large bowl. Add the cumin, paprika, cinnamon, black pepper, and cayenne pepper and stir until the spices are well-blended into the yogurt.
2. Cut each chicken thigh into 4 pieces and add the pieces to the yogurt mixture and mix until the chicken pieces are well-coated with the mixture. Allow the chicken to marinate for 30 minutes or more in the refrigerator.
3. Remove the chicken from the marinade and place in a single layer in the air fryer basket. Set the air fryer to 370ºF and cook the chicken for 10 minutes.
4. Open the air fryer and flip over the chicken. Set the air fryer to 370ºF and cook again for another 5 minutes.
5. Test with a meat thermometer to ensure the chicken has reached an internal temperature of 150ºF.
6. Serve and enjoy.

NUTRITIONAL FACTS (Per Serving)

- 290 calories; 3g net carbs; 23g fat; 20g protein.

Air Fried Buttered-Shrimp with Chicken Stock

Prep Time: 5 mins; Cook Time: 10 mins; Total Time: 15 mins.

Yield: 4 Portions.

INGREDIENTS

- 1 pound (frozen) shrimp, defrosted
- 4 tablespoons butter
- 2 tablespoons Chicken Stock
- 1 tablespoon lemon juice
- 2 teaspoons red pepper flakes
- 1 teaspoon dried chives
- 1 tablespoon minced garlic
- 1 teaspoon dried basil

INSTRUCTIONS

1. Place a metal pan that can fit your air fryer into your air fryer and preheat your air fryer to 330F for 2-3 minutes.
2. Place the butter, garlic, and red pepper flakes into the hot pan.
3. Allow it to cook for 2 minutes, stirring once, until the butter has melted.
4. Open the air fryer, add all ingredients to the pan, stirring gently.
5. Allow shrimp to cook for 5 minutes, stirring once. At this point, the butter should be well-melted and liquid, bathing the shrimp in spiced goodness.
6. Mix very well, remove the pan using silicone mitts, and let it rest for 1 minute on the counter while shrimp cook in the residual heat. You're doing this so that you let the.
7. Stir at the end of the minute and remove from the air fryer.

NUTRITIONAL FACTS (Per Serving)

- ✓ 284 calories; 4g carbs; 25g fat; 19g protein.

Air Fried Scallops with Basil

Prep Time: 5 mins; Cook Time: 10 mins; Total Time: 15 mins.

Yield: 2 Servings.

INGREDIENTS

- ❖ 1 tablespoon chopped fresh basil
- ❖ scallops
- ❖ 3/4 cup heavy whipping cream
- ❖ 1 tablespoon tomato paste
- ❖ 1 teaspoon minced garlic
- ❖ 1/2 teaspoon salt
- ❖ 1/2 teaspoon ground black pepper
- ❖ 1 12-ounce package frozen spinach thawed and drained
- ❖ Cooking Oil Spray

INGREDIENTS

1. Spray a 7-inch heatproof pan, and place the spinach in an even layer at the bottom.
2. Spray both sides of the scallops with vegetable oil, and season with little salt and pepper, and place scallops in the pan on top of the spinach.
3. Mix together the cream, tomato paste, basil, garlic, salt, and pepper In a small bowl and pour over the spinach and scallops.

4. Set the air fryer to 350F for 10 minutes until the scallops are cooked through to an internal temperature of 135F and the sauce is hot and bubbling.
5. Serve immediately.

NUTRITIONAL FACTS (Per Serving)
- ✓ 97 calories; 3g fat; 19.5g carbs; 4g protein.

Air Fryer Herbed Tandoori Chicken

Prep Time: 30 mins; Cook Time: 15 mins; Total Time: 45 mins.

Yield: 4 Servings.

INGREDIENTS
- ❖ 1 pound chicken tenders each cut in half
- ❖ 1/4 cup Greek yogurt
- ❖ 1 tablespoon minced ginger
- ❖ 1 tablespoon minced garlic
- ❖ 1/4 cup parsley
- ❖ 1 teaspoon salt
- ❖ 1/2 teaspoon cayenne
- ❖ 1 teaspoon turmeric
- ❖ 1 teaspoon garam masala
- ❖ 1 teaspoon smoked paprika
- ❖ 1 tablespoon ghee
- ❖ 2 teaspoons lemon juice
- ❖ 2 tablespoons chopped cilantro

INSTRUCTIONS
1. In a bowl, mix all ingredients except the ghee, lemon juice, and cilantro.
2. Preheat your air fryer for 5 minutes.
3. Open up the air fryer and carefully lay the tandoori chicken in a single layer in the basket of your air fryer.
4. Using a silicone brush, baste the chicken with ghee on one side And air fry on 350F for 10 minutes.
5. Remove and flip over the chicken, and baste on the other side,
6. Cook for another 5 minutes. Cook a meat thermometer reads an internal temperature of 165F.

7. Remove and place on a serving plate. Add lemon juice and mix, and garnish with cilantro and serve.

NUTRITIONAL FACTS (Per Serving)

- ✓ 324 calories; 5g carbs; 28g fat; 20g protein.

Air Fried Chicken Coconut Meatballs Recipe

Prep Time: 10 mins; Cook Time: 12 mins; Total Time: 23 mins.

Yield: 4 Servings.

INGREDIENTS

- ❖ 1/4 cup unsweetened coconut, shredded
- ❖ 1 pound ground chicken
- ❖ 2 Green Onions finely chopped
- ❖ 1 tablespoon soy sauce
- ❖ 1/2 cup chopped cilantro
- ❖ 1 teaspoon sriracha sauce
- ❖ 1 teaspoon sesame oil
- ❖ 1 tablespoon hoisin sauce
- ❖ Salt to taste
- ❖ Ground black pepper to taste

INSTRUCTIONS

1. Preheat your air fryer to 350F.
2. Prepare a large bowl and combine all the ingredients in it. Mix together to form a wet sticky mixture.
3. Line a cookie sheet with aluminum foil and scoop rounds of the mixture onto the foil.
4. Carefully arrange them in the air fryer and cook for 10 minutes, flipping once, until they reach an internal temperature of 165F. You may need to work in batches.
5. Let cool then serve.

NUTRITIONAL FACTS (Per Serving)

- ✓ 387calories; 14 carbs; 34g fat; 20g protein.

Air Fried Salad with Greek Yoghurt & Roasted Pepper Dressing

Prep Time: 15 mins; Cook Time: 10 mins; Total Time: 25 mins.

Yield: 4 Portions.

INGREDIENTS
- 3 tablespoons Greek yogurt
- 1 large head rocket leaves
- 1 red bell pepper

For the Dressing
- 1 tablespoon lemon juice
- 1 romaine lettuce, in broad strips
- 2 tablespoons olive oil
- Freshly ground black pepper to taste
- Salt to taste

INSTRUCTIONS
1. Preheat the air fryer to 400°F.
2. Place the bell pepper in your air fryer basket and slide the basket into the air fryer. Set the timer to 10 minutes and roast the bell pepper until the skin becomes slightly burnt and blackened.
3. Put the bell pepper in a bowl covered for 12 minutes.
4. Then slice the bell pepper into four sections and remove the seeds and the skin. Cut into strips and set aside.
5. Prepare the dressing. Place 2 tablespoons of the moisture from the bell pepper in a medium bowl, add the lemon juice, the yogurt, and the olive oil. Season with pepper and salt to taste.
6. Toss the lettuce and the rocket leaves in the dressing, and garnish the salad with the bell pepper strips and serve.

NUTRITIONAL FACTS (Per Serving)
- **109 calories; 7g carbs; g 7fat; 6g protein.**

Air Fried Mini Frankfurters Pastry with Mustard

Prep Time: 10 mins; Cook Time: 20 mins; Total Time: 30 mins,

Yield: 3 Servings,

INGREDIENTS
- 1 tin mini Frankfurters
- 1 tablespoon fine mustard, more for garnish
- 100 g (chilled, defrosted) ready-made puff pastry

INSTRUCTIONS
1. Drain the sausages completely and pat them dry with kitchen paper.
2. Cut the pastry into strips and coat the strips with a thin layer of mustard.
3. Roll each sausage spirally into a strip of pastry.
4. Put half the sausages in pastry in your air fryer basket and air fry on 400F for 10 minutes or until golden brown. Repeat steps for the remaining half of the sausages.
5. Place the sausages in a platter, garnish with mustard and enjoy.

NUTRITIONAL FACTS (Per Serving)
- 151 calories; 10g fat; 9g net carbs; 8g protein.

Air Fryer Zucchini Turkey Burgers Recipe

Prep Time: 10 mins; Cook Time: 10 mins; Total Time: 20 mins.

Yield: 5 Portions.

INGREDIENTS
- 1 pound lean ground turkey
- 6 ounces grated zucchini
- 1/4 cup breadcrumbs
- 1 tablespoon red onion, grated
- 1 tsp kosher salt to taste
- 1 clove minced garlic
- Fresh ground pepper to taste
- Oil spray

INSTRUCTIONS

1. Squeeze out all the moisture from the zucchini using kitchen paper.
2. Combine all the ingredients in a large bowl. Mix well until completely combined. Make 5 equal patties from the mixture, 4 oz each and 1/2 inch thick.
3. Preheat your air fryer to 370F.
4. Divide patties into two batches. Arrange the first batch of patties in a single layer in your air fryer basket. Set the timer to 10 minutes and cook, turning halfway until browned and cooked through in the center. Do same for the second batch of patties or burgers.
5. Enjoy.

NUTRITIONAL FACTS (Per Serving)

- ✓ 351 calories; 20 carbs; 16g fat; 28g protein.

Air Fryer Avocado Fries with Lime Sauce

Prep Time: 7 mins; Cook Time: 8 mins; Total Time: 15 mins.

Yield: 4 Servings.

INGREDIENTS

- ❖ 2 small avocados (4 oz each), peeled, pitted and cut into 16 wedges
- ❖ 1 large egg, lightly beaten
- ❖ 3/4 cup gluten-free breadcrumbs
- ❖ 1 1/4 teaspoons of lime chili seasoning salt
- ❖ For the lime sauce
- ❖ 1/4 cup Greek Yogurt
- ❖ 3 tablespoons light mayonnaise
- ❖ 2 teaspoons fresh lime juice
- ❖ 1/8 teaspoon kosher salt

INSTRUCTIONS

1. Preheat your air-fryer to 390F for 2 minutes.
2. Prepare two small shallow bowls. Place egg in one of the bowls and in the other bowl, combine breadcrumbs with 1 teaspoon lime chili seasoning salt.
3. Season avocado wedges with remaining lime chili seasoning salt. Dip each piece first in egg, and then in breadcrumbs.

4. Spray both sides with oil then transfer to the air fryer and air fry for 8 minutes, turning halfway through.
5. Serve hot with lime dipping sauce.

NUTRITIONAL FACTS (Per Serving)
- ✓ 197 calories; 7g protein; 10g net carbs; 13g fat.

Air Fried Lamb Meatballs with Lemon Peel & Greek Feta

Prep Time: 10 mins; Cook Time: 8 mins; Total Time: 18 mins.
Yield: 10 Persons.

INGREDIENTS
- ❖ 1 cup minced lamb
- ❖ 1 slice of stale white bread, turned into crumbs
- ❖ 50 g Greek feta, crumbled
- ❖ 1 tablespoon fresh oregano, chopped
- ❖ ½ tablespoon grated lemon peel
- ❖ Freshly ground black pepper

INSTRUCTIONS
1. Preheat the air fryer to 400°F for 2 minutes.
2. Combine the lamb with the bread crumbs, feta, oregano, lemon peel and black pepper in a bowl, evenly kneading all ingredients together.
3. Divide the mince into 10 equal portions, and using damp hands, form smooth balls.
4. Put the balls in a pan that can fit into your air fryer and place in your air fryer basket. Set the timer to 8 minutes and cook until the balls are brown and done.
5. Serve the meatballs hot on a platter and enjoy.

NUTRITIONAL FACTS (Per Serving)
- ✓ 181 calories; 7g carbs; 16g fat; 14g protein.

Air Fried Crispy Bacon Wrapped Scallops

Prep Time: 5 mins; Cook Time: 20 mins; Total Time: 25 mins.

Yield: 4 Servings.

INGREDIENTS

- 16 large sea scallops, cleaned and pat dry with paper towels
- slices center-cut bacon
- 16 toothpicks
- Olive oil spray
- Freshly ground black pepper, to taste

INSTRUCTIONS

1. Preheat air fryer to 400F.
2. Place the bacon in the air fryer and cook for 3 minutes, turning halfway through. Remove and let cool for some minutes.
3. After cooling, pat the scallops dry using paper towels.
4. Wrap each scallop in a slice of bacon and secure it with a toothpick.
5. Spread olive oil over the bacon-wrapped scallops and sprinkle with some pepper.
6. Arrange scallops in a single layer in the air fryer, cook, in batches 8 minutes each, turning halfway until scallop is tender and bacon is cooked through.
7. Serve warm and enjoy.

NUTRITIONAL FACTS (Per Serving)

- **224 calories; 2g carbs; 17g fat; 12g protein.**

Air Fried Beef Bulgogi Burgers with Scallions & Gochujang

Prep Time: 15 mins; Cook Time: 10 mins; Total Time: 25 mins.

Yield: 4 Servings.

INGREDIENTS

- 2 tablespoon gochujang
- 1 tablespoon dark soy sauce
- 2 teaspoon minced garlic

- 2 teaspoon minced ginger
- 2 teaspoon sugar
- 1 pound lean ground beef
- 1 tablespoon Sesame Oil
- 1/4 cup Green Onions
- 1/2 teaspoon salt
- 1/4 cup mayonnaise
- 1 tablespoon sesame Oil
- 2 teaspoon sesame Seeds
- 1/4 cup scallions chopped
- 4 hamburger buns
- 1 tablespoon gochujang

INSTRUCTIONS

1. In a large bowl, mix ground beef, gochujang, soy sauce, garlic, ginger, sugar, sesame oil, chopped onions, and salt and refrigerate the mixture for at least 30 minutes.
2. Divide the meat into four portions and form round patties, creating a slight depression in the middle.
3. Set your air fryer to 360F and place the patties in a single layer in the air fryer basket and air fry for 10 minutes.
4. While the patties cook, mix together the mayonnaise, gochujang, sesame oil, sesame seeds, and scallions.
5. Using a meat thermometer, ensure that the meat has reached an internal temperature of 160F then transfer to a serving dish.
6. Serve the patties with hamburger buns and the gochujang mayonnaise. Enjoy!

NUTRITIONAL FACTS (Per Serving)

- ✓ 353 calories; 19 carbs; 16g fat; 28g protein.

Air Fryer Parmesan Scotch Eggs

Prep Time: 20 mins; Cook Time: 25 mins; Total Time: 45 mins.

Yield: 4 Servings.

INGREDIENTS

- 1 cup shredded parmesan cheese
- 1 tablespoon fresh chives finely chopped
- 4 eggs, hard-boiled, peeled

- 2 tablespoons fresh parsley finely chopped
- 1/8 teaspoon grated nutmeg
- 1/8 teaspoon sea salt
- 1/8 teaspoon ground black pepper
- 1 pound pork sausage
- 2 teaspoons coarse-ground mustard

INSTRUCTIONS

1. Combine the sausage, mustard, chives, parsley, nutmeg, salt, and black pepper in a large bowl. Gently mix until everything is well combined. Shape mixture into four equal-size patties.
2. Place each egg on a sausage patty and shape sausage around egg. Dip each in shredded Parmesan cheese to cover completely, pressing lightly to adhere.
3. Arrange eggs in your air fryer basket. Spray lightly with oil. Set fryer to 400°F and cook patties for 15 minutes. Turn eggs halfway through and spray with oil.
4. Serve garnished with coarse-ground mustard.

NUTRITIONAL FACTS (Per Serving)

- ✓ 307 calories; 19g carbs; 9g fat; 22g protein.

Air Fried Roasted Asparagus and Avocado Soup Recipe

Prep Time: 10 mins; Cook Time: 10 mins; Total time: 20 mins.

Yield: 4 Servings.

INGREDIENTS

- ounces asparagus
- 1 tablespoon garlic-infused olive oil
- 2 cups chicken stock
- 1/2 lemon juiced
- 1 tablespoon ghee
- Fine sea salt to taste
- fresh ground pepper to taste
- 1 avocado peeled and cubed

INSTRUCTIONS

1. Preheat your air fryer to 390F.
2. Toss asparagus with garlic-infused olive oil, salt and pepper and roast for 10 minutes.
3. Carefully transfer asparagus to a high-speed blender with remaining ingredients and puree until smooth. Add salt and pepper.
4. Add water to desired consistency, if needed, and warm gently over medium heat. Serve hot and enjoy.

NUTRITIONAL FACTS (Per Serving)

- ✓ **200 calories; 8g carbs; 16g fat; 6g protein.**

Vegan Air fried Roasted Garlic Recipe

Prep Time: 5 mins; Cook Time: 20 mins; Total Time: 25 mins.

Yield: 4 Portions.

INGREDIENTS

- ❖ 1 medium-sized head garlic
- ❖ 2 teaspoons extra virgin olive oil

INSTRUCTIONS

1. Remove any excess papery peel from a head of garlic but still leave each clove covered.
2. Cut 1/4 inch off the top of a head of garlic, exposing the tops of the cloves underneath.
3. Drizzle extra virgin olive oil onto the exposed parts of the cloves.
4. Wrap the head of garlic in aluminum foil and put it into your air fryer and cook at 400F for 20-25 minutes until cooked through.
5. Remove from the air fryer and allow it to cool.
6. Once it is cool, gently squeeze on each clove, and it will pop right out of its skin.
7. Serve the roasted garlic with pizza as a topping if desired.

NUTRITIONAL FACTS (Per Serving)

- ✓ **16 calories; 1g carbs; 3g fat; 0g protein.**

Air Fryer Brown Loaf with Sunflower Seeds

Prep Time: 40 mins; Cook Time: 20 mins; Total Time: 1 hour.
Yield: 4 Servings.

INGREDIENTS
- 100 g whole wheat flour
- 100 g plain flour
- 7g nutritional yeast
- 1 cup lukewarm water
- 50 g sunflower seeds
- 1 teaspoon kosher salt

INSTRUCTIONS
1. Combine both flours in a bowl with salt and mix. Add the yeast and the seeds, stir to combine. While stirring, add 1 cup lukewarm water and mix until the dough forms a soft ball.
2. Knead the dough for about 5 minutes until it becomes smooth and elastic. Then shape it into a ball and place in a bowl. Cover the bowl with plastic wrap or lid and allow it to rise in a warm place for about 30 minutes.
3. Preheat your air fryer to 400°F. Brush the top of the dough with water.
4. Put a small cake pan (must fit into your air fryer) in the fryer basket and slide the basket into the air fryer. Set the timer to 18 minutes and bake the bread until it is golden brown and done. Allow the bread to cool on a wire rack. Serve.

NUTRITIONAL FACTS (Per Serving)
- 109 calories; 11g carbs; 7g fat; 9g protein.

Air fryer Ratatouille Recipe

Prep time: 10 mins; Cook Time: 15 mins; Total Time: 25 mins.
Yield: 4 Servings.

INGREDIENTS
- ounces zucchini
- 1 yellow bell pepper
- ounces eggplant
- 2 tomatoes

- ❖ 1 onion, peeled
- ❖ 1 clove garlic, crushed
- ❖ 2 teaspoons dried Provençal herbs
- ❖ Salt to taste
- ❖ Freshly ground black pepper to taste
- ❖ 1 tablespoon olive oil

INSTRUCTIONS

1. Slice the zucchini, eggplant, bell pepper, tomatoes, and onion.
2. Place the vegetables in a bowl and mix in the garlic, Provencal herbs, olive, salt, and pepper.
3. Put the bowl in the basket and slide the basket into the air fryer and air fry for 15 minutes on 392°F, stirring halfway through.
4. When done cooking, serve a cutlet and enjoy.

NUTRITIONAL FACTS (Per Serving)

✓ 79 calories; 6g carbs; 3.8g fat; 2g protein.

Air Fried Roasted Oregano Pepper Rolls with Feta Cheese

Prep Time: 25 mins; Cook Time: 10 mins; Total Time: 35 mins.

Yield: 8 Portions.

INGREDIENTS

- ❖ 2 large red and orange bell peppers
- ❖ Feta with green onion Crumble
- ❖ 3/4 cup Greek feta cheese, crumbled
- ❖ 1 green onion, thinly sliced
- ❖ 2 tablespoons oregano, finely chopped

INSTRUCTIONS

1. Preheat your air fryer to 400°F for 2 minutes.
2. Put the bell peppers in the basket of the air fryer. Set your air fryer timer to 10 minutes and cook the peppers until the skin is slightly charred.

3. Meanwhile, place the cheese in a small bowl and mix in the onion slices and chopped oregano.
4. When done cooking peppers, remove from the air fryer and allow it to cool. Halve the peppers lengthwise and remove the seeds and the skin.
5. Coat the pepper pieces with the feta mixture and roll them up, starting from the narrowest end.
6. Secure the rolls with tapas forks or toothpick and place them on a plate.

NUTRITIONAL FACTS (Per Serving)

✓ 130 calories; 6g carbs; 7g fat; 4g protein.

Air fryer Crispy Roasted Onion Potatoes

Prep Time: 3 mins; Cook Time: 20 mins; Total Time: 23 mins.

Yield: 4 Servings.

INGREDIENTS

- 2 pounds baby red potatoes, peeled and quartered
- 2 tablespoons olive oil
- 1 envelope Lipton onion soup mix

INSTRUCTIONS

1. Preheat air fryer to 400F.
2. Place the potatoes in a medium bowl and mix in olive oil.
3. Add the onion soup mix and stir until all the potatoes are well coated.
4. Add the potatoes to the air fryer basket and cook for about 20 minutes or until potatoes are tender and golden brown, stirring the potatoes halfway through.
5. Serve and enjoy!

NUTRITIONAL FACTS (Per Serving)

✓ 308 calories; 45g carbs; 7g fat; 13g protein.

Air Fried Chocolate Cake with Cocoa Powder

Prep Time: 15 mins; Cook Time: 30 mins; Total Time: 45 mins.

Yield: 8 Servings.

INGREDIENTS

For the Cake

- 3 eggs
- 1 cup sour cream
- 1 1/4 cup flour
- 150g caster sugar
- 40g cocoa powder
- 1 1/2 teaspoons baking powder
- 125g unsalted butter
- 2 teaspoon vanilla essence

For the Chocolate icing

- 150g chocolate
- 50g unsalted softened butter
- 200g icing sugar
- 1 teaspoon vanilla essence

INSTRUCTIONS

1. Preheat your air fryer to 320F.
2. Place all the cake ingredients into a blender and blend well. Transfer to an oven dish.
3. Place the oven dish into the basket of your air fryer. Slide the basket into the air fryer and air fry the cake for 25-30 minutes until cooked through.
4. Remove the dish from the basket and leave the cake on a wire rack to cool.
5. Meanwhile, melt the chocolate in the microwave. Leave to cool a little, then mix all of the icing ingredients together. Remove the cooled cake from the oven dish and transfer it to a serving plate. Cover the cake with the chocolate icing and serve.

NUTRITIONAL FACTS (Per Serving)

- **214 calories; 23g carbs; 12g fat; 4g protein.**

Air Fried Feta Triangles with Green Onion Recipe

Prep Time: 20 mins; Cook Time: 9 mins; Total Time: 29 mins.

Yield: 3 portions.

INGREDIENTS

- 100 g feta
- 2 tablespoons flat-leafed parsley, finely chopped
- 1 green onion, finely sliced into rings
- 1 egg yolk
- Freshly ground black pepper to taste
- 5 sheets of frozen filo pastry, defrosted
- Oil for brushing

INSTRUCTIONS

1. Whisk the egg yolk in a bowl and mix in the feta, parsley and green onion and season with pepper.
2. Cut each sheet of filo pastry into three strips.
3. Put a full teaspoon of the feta mixture on the underside of a strip of pastry. Fold the tip of the pastry over the filling to form a triangle, folding the strip zigzag until the filling is wrapped up in a triangle of pastry. Repeat instructions with the other strips of pastry with feta.
4. Preheat the air fryer to 400°F.
5. Brush the triangles with oil and place five triangles in the basket. Slide the basket into the air fryer and air fry for 3 minutes. Repeat steps for remaining feta triangles. Transfer to a platter and serve.

NUTRITIONAL FACTS (Per Serving)

- ✓ 140 calories; 11g carbs; 7g fat; 11g protein.

Keto Air Fried Meatloaf Sliders Recipe

Prep Time: 10 mins; Cook Time: 10 mins; Total Time: 20 mins.

Yield: 8 Servings.

INGREDIENTS

- 2 eggs beaten
- 1/4 cup onion, finely chopped
- 1 clove garlic, minced
- 1/2 cup extra fine blanched almond flour
- 1/4 cup coconut flour
- 1/4 cup ketchup
- 1/2 teaspoon sea salt
- 1/2 teaspoon black pepper
- 1 teaspoon Italian Seasoning
- 1 tablespoon Worcestershire Sauce
- 1/2 teaspoon dried Tarragon
- 1 lb ground beef
- Lettuce wraps for serving, optional

INSTRUCTIONS

1. In a large mixing bowl, combine all the ingredients and mix well. From the mixture, make patties with similar size (I used patties that are 2 inches in diameter and 1 inch thick). Place the patties on a platter and let them rest for about 10 minutes in the refrigerator.
2. Meanwhile, preheat your air fryer to 360°F.
3. Place the patties in the air fryer basket and cook for 10 minutes, flipping halfway through cook time.
4. Remove patties from air fryer and transfer to a serving plate and cover until all the patties are cooked. Work in batches if necessary.
5. Serve sliders on lettuce wraps and enjoy.

NUTRITIONAL FACTS (Per Serving)

- **228 calories; 6g carbs; 2g fiber; 16g fat and 12g protein.**

Vegan Air Fried Crispy Ravioli Recipe

Prep Time: 15 mins; Cook Time: 8 mins; Total Time: 23 mins.

Yield: 4 Servings.

INGREDIENTS

- 1/2 cup bread crumbs
- 2 teaspoons nutritional yeast flakes
- 1 teaspoon dried basil
- 1 teaspoon dried oregano
- 1 teaspoon garlic powder
- Pinch salt & pepper
- 1/4 cup aquafaba liquid
- ounces thawed vegan ravioli
- Spritz cooking spray
- 1/2 cup marinara for dipping

INSTRUCTIONS

1. Combine the bread crumbs, flakes, and basil on a plate. Mix in oregano, garlic powder, salt, and pepper.
2. Place aquafaba into another bowl.
3. Dip ravioli into aquafaba, shake off excess liquid and then dip also in bread crumb mixture. Make sure that the ravioli is evenly coated. Continue the procedure until all the ravioli is coated.
4. Then arrange the ravioli in your air fryer basket without overlapping. You may want to cook in batches if necessary.
5. Spritz the ravioli with cooking spray. Turn air fryer to 390F and air fry for 6 minutes. Carefully flip over halfway through and continue to cook for 2 more minutes.
6. Remove ravioli from the air fryer, transfer to a serving platter and enjoy with warm marinara for dipping.

NUTRITIONAL FACTS (Per Serving)

- 150 calories; 27g carbs; 3g fiber; 5g protein.

Air Fried Bratwurst with Crusty Bread Rolls Recipe

Prep Time: 10 mins; Cook Time: 30 mins; Total Time: 40 mins.

Yield: 4 Portions.

INGREDIENTS
- 4 brown crusty bread rolls
- 1 2/3 cups flour, sifted
- Dried yeast
- 2 teaspoons salt
- 3 tablespoons sugar
- 20g baking powder
- 1 cup warm water
- 4 Bratwurst
- 1 egg yolk, whisked
- 2 teaspoons coarse sea salt, more for sprinkling

INSTRUCTIONS
1. In a mixing bowl, combine the flour, egg, yeast, salt, sugar, baking powder and warm water. Mix to form a dough.
2. Divide the dough into four equal pieces and shape each part into a ball. Let the balls rest for 10 minutes then roll them out in three stages to form pencil-like strands. Leave a break of 10 minutes between each stage.
3. Make the strands into pretzel shapes and boil them in a pan with water and 3 tablespoons of baking powder for one minute. Sprinkle with salt.
4. Heat your air fryer to 356F and air fry the pretzel for 10 minutes until brown and crispy. Increase air fryer to 400F, place the bread rolls and bratwursts in the air fryer and cook for 8 minutes.

NUTRITIONAL FACTS (Per Serving)
- 109 calories; 13g carbs; 7g fat; 10g protein.

CONCLUSION

The air fryer is an easy modern tool that cooks all your favorite food. Cooking using an air fryer is much healthier than cooking your food with a deep fryer. This is because it requires a lot less oil to cook the food. Luckily, you'll still get all of the great tastes you love in your favorite fried foods without the fat.

Hot air frying is much safer. Deep fat frying causes over 1,000 casualties every year. All these can be eliminated by air frying. The air fryer can easily be operated even by young teenagers within the home. If you need safety, economy, health, and convenience, then air frying is the way to go.

THE END

Made in the USA
Middletown, DE
27 December 2019